BUDDHIST MONASTIC ARCHITECTURE
IN SRI LANKA
(The Woodland Shrines)

BUDDHIST MONASTIC ARCHITECTURE
IN SRI LANKA
(The Woodland Shrines)

Anuradha Seneviratna
Benjamin Polk

abhinav publications

First published in India 1992

Publishers
Shakti Malik
Abhinav Publications
E-37, Hauz Khas
New Delhi-110 016

ISBN 81-7017-281-0

Text printed at
Mehta Offset Works
Mehta House
16-A, Naraina II
New Delhi-110 028

PREFACE

Little attention has been given by most scholars to the dominant role of timber construction in Sri Lanka's ancient architecture. In doing so, this book presents a hitherto unappreciated facet of South Asian cultural achievement. At the same time our account leads on with a light touch appropriate to on-site trips in the Kandyan Hills.

We give our story of searching out of the picturesque wood buildings of the Buddhist monastic centres in the central hills of Sri Lanka. Our presentation revolves around colour photographs of village temples and other monuments taken by architect Benjamin Polk in 1980-81. It is concerned with an architecture that reflects in popular traditions the great heritage of Monsoon Asia that emanated from India, Nepal, and Southeast Asia.

The guiding hand of Anuradha Seneviratna brings it first-hand authority and historical detail, and Benjamin Polk's twelve-year architectural experience in the countries of South Asia gives it its architectural focus.

Emily Polk, poet and painter, who has also published on Asian subjects (*Delhi, Old and New*, Rand McNally, and *Poems and Epigrams*, Rupa, Calcutta), has researched the old records and writings from early Sri Lankan history and travel, and has put those threads of adventure into this present form, and she has given the text a dramatic flair throughout. The full flavour of daily life is evoked in her Epilogue.

For the first time colour photographs of the ancient wood buildings appear under one cover, presented comprehensively along with currents of often little-known Sri Lankan history. The buildings, as noted, are, except for the great Temple of the Tooth in Kandy, close to folk architecture, and in their structural essentials resemble village houses. They represent the dominant building type in the widespread area of rice-growing, bamboo-using Buddhist lands. Their form and aesthetics reflect the ceremonies appropriate to the housing of the image of the Buddha, and this function is the single key to the building program.

The book can be seen as a traveller's reference guide to the Hill Country as it was before the recent tragic strife. It displays our delight in discovering new aspects of a relatively little known area — one that is quite essentially South Asian. Architectural observation is interwoven with parallel description of the drama of the land and its people.

For further analysis of religious and architectural problems the reader is especially referred to Anagarika B. Govinda's "Some Aspects of Stupa Symbolism", Kitabistan Press, Allahabad and London, 1940, and to L.K. Karunaratne's "The Wooden Architecture of Sri Lanka", The Ceylon Historical Journal, October 1978.

The first three chapters set the stage for the subject of the book: Buddhist monastic architecture of the central hills, and the Architectural Note briefly sketches our own direction in this survey of about thirty buildings.

CONTENTS

CHAPTER I

TRAVELLING IS VICTORY

(Arab Proverb)

Ten years have passed since we saw far below us the shadow of our plane racing over the ocean like the ghost of a clipper ship haunting its old route to Sri Lanka. Just ahead a low horizon of land appears, then sand flats, round as coins, half submerged in the shallows. The name of the island was pronounced (and spelt) *Ceylon* when James Emerson Tennant sailed to Sri Lanka in 1845: "Ceylon, from whatever direction it is approached unfolds a scene of loveliness and grandeur unsurpassed by any land in the universe. The traveller...or the adventurer from Europe, recently inured to the sands of Egypt and the scorched headlands of Arabia, is alike enthralled by the vision of beauty which expands before him as the island rises from the sea, its lofty mountains coverd by luxuriant forests, and its shores, till they meet the ripple of the waves, bright with the foliage of perpetual spring."

Idyllic! but this is 1980: we are approaching from the *sky* at 300 hundred miles *an hour*, a direction and a speed undreamed of then; we have no time for a glimpse of the "vision of beauty"; we fasten our belts, clutch the arms of the seats, murmur a reverent "LandHo!" saluting the past, and roll on to the tarmac at Sri Lanka's airport.

"Travelling is victory." Travel these days for a change of scene is victory over boredom. Edification seldom enters into it. But "restlessness and groping are among men's legacies." Victory for those who went to sea in the early days, for the wide ranging Arabs who coined the proverb, was over Fate: winds, uncharted rocks, unstable ships and faulty seamanship. Sea travellers then, and traders too for their own reasons, ran these calculated risks to learn about the world. They learned about Sri Lanka. "There is no island in the world, Great Britain itself not excepted, that has attracted the attention of authors in so many distant ages", writes Emerson Tennant. "There is no nation in ancient...times possessed of a language and a literature, the writers of which have not at some time made it their theme."

Sri Lanka has two histories: her ocean links with the world; and the struggles of her inland kingdoms.

The record of her ocean history begins in BC 323 in the log book of Onesicritus, Alexander's Admiral of fleet, with a description of Taprobane (the *e* was sounded) — this is the name given the island by the Macedonians. Pliny writes about it: "It had been long time thought by men in ancient days that Taprobane was a second world, in such sort that many have taken it to be the place of the Antipodes calling it the Antichthonic world. But after the time of Alexander the Great, and the voyage of his army into those parts, it was discovered and known for a truth, both that it was an island and what compass it bears."

The unwritten history of seafaring — heroic tales and racial legends – implies that long before BC 1500 Far Eastern and Middle Eastern traders were sailing past Sri Lanka, coasting to and from the Erythraean Sea, the gateway to the Mediterranean now separately called the Red and Arabian Seas. King Solomon dispatched a fleet every three years to bring "gold, silver, ivory, apes and peacocks" from the Far East. The round trip to China on a port-to-port "coaster" took longer than that; the captains stayed in sight of land, dropped anchor at safe roadsteads, went ashore for food and water and to trade.

In the more recent past a few highly civilized societies looked upon trade as an inferior occupation; however some anthropologists believe that trade may be the primary civilizing impulse. Children trade pebbles for shells, boys trade new bikes for old — the human impulse for trade is an instinct so ingrained and unquenchable that in pursuing it primitive men overcame their natural fear of the sea. There was no need to go to sea, inland trading-tribes mingled freely. Although boat travel was easier than land travel, and rivers, lakes and shallow coastal waters were safe thoroughfares for the first dugout boats or rafts of reeds lashed in bundles together — one primitive tribe could put 60 men for a short sea trip on a raft of flax flower stems floating on sea-kelp bladders — relatively few men left terra firma for the chancy life of a sea trade. Only those took to the waves who were urged on by daring temperaments and higher quotas of curiosity; astronauts of their day, they began *our* journey into space. We do not know what we are looking for in space, but like the first exploring sea traders we are exceptionally curious, and discoveries will be made we are not looking for — curiosity can be the prelude to useful accidents.

In AD 51, a Greek captain collecting taxes for the Romans along the shores of the Red Sea was caught by a monsoon and blown to

Taprobane "in such wise driven by the north winds...for a space of fifteen days that in the end he fell in with a harbour thereof..."

How many sailors in small coasting craft caught in these cyclonic winds lost their lives before this man survived? The Fates gave him his victory and with it a gift for the world: the seasonal monsoon was revealed as a force that could be harnessed. "This discovery", says a historian, "caused a revolution in the art of navigation and trade between Europe and Asia." In the following centuries the seafaring races would build sailing ships that could withstand the open sea, and chart ocean trade routes. Those to the East centred on Sri Lanka. A Greek merchant from Alexandria sailed to Taprobane in AD 545. "The island being as it is, in a central position, is much frequented by ships from all parts...(even) the remote parts...China and other trading places." In 500 years the Eastern world had mastered the art of sailing before the great winds.

By the Middle Ages the "Moors" — Moroccans, Persians and Arabs were all Muslims and were called Moors by the Portuguese— had a virtual monopoly on the island's spice and gem trade, but not until Marco Polo, returning home by sea in 1293 after twenty-three years in China, stopped at the island for a few days, was the splendour in its full flavour revealed to Europe. "This, for its actual size, is better circumstanced than any other island in the world...(and) produced more beautiful and valuable rubies than are found in any other part of the world, and likewise sapphires, topazes, amethysts, garnets and many other precious and costly stones. The king is supposed to possess the grandest ruby that ever was seen, being a span in length and the thickness of a man's arm, brilliant beyond description and without a single flaw. It has the appearance of a glowing fire...The Grand Khan, Kublai, sent ambassadors to the monarch, with a request that he would yield to him the possession of this ruby; in return for which he should receive the value of a city. The answer he made was to this effect: he would not sell it for the treasure of the universe..."

Ibn Batuta, a rich young Moor from Tangiers, lived in the spirit of the age. In 1328 at the age of 25 he determined "to travel through the earth". By 1342 he had married several wives and reached the Indian Ocean. Hiring a ship and provisions for the three day voyage, but with an unskilled captain, he beat up-wind from the Maldives to Sri Lanka. The captain lost his way..."We were nine days under sail and on the ninth we...perceived the islands of Serendib raised in the air like a column of smoke" — the southern mountains of Sri Lanka. The Arab name for the island was Serendib. The Fates were fond of Ibn Batuta; he travelled for 28 years covering 75,000 miles, wrote his adventures at 55 and lived to be 69. This was a triumph then when a man of action seldom lived beyond 40.

Realities of life under sail in the Middle Ages seemed incredible to the point of absurdity to the sophisticates of the Age of Reason. By his mimicry and parody of old sea stories of hurricanes, wrecks, crazed sailors and mutinies, Swift conjured up a ridiculing mood for his savage fables. Although he lampooned nautical language, the tales he laughed at were not exaggerations. Medieval seafaring was carried on against the odds of a daily game of Russian roulette. The seafarers, men very like Gulliver "Having been condemned by Nature and Fortune to an active and restless life (their) thirst...of seeing the world, notwithstanding... past misfortunes, continuing as violent as ever", were hard-living romantics who believed everything they heard and imagined more than they saw. But threads of fact are woven into their memoirs and drawings of sea serpents, fabulous beasts, two-headed men "and men whose heads do grow beneath their shoulders"...strange creatures live in the deep valleys of the oceans and sometimes wash ashore; in the jungles of that day — who knows — there may have been primitive proto-men with sloping necks, or with extremely long and bulbous craniums, their hair hanging over their eyes. Upright, round headed modern men would describe them just that way.

Marco Polo and Ibn Batuta and other writing travellers with a "thirst for seeing the world" stirred up a 15th century equivalent of our tourist rush; Portugal's Henry the Navigator sent ships to gain possessions in Asia; Christopher Columbus, sailing from Spain, discovered America; trading companies were formed and ships built, their numbers attracting pirates who with their western cousins the buccaneers hunted the trade seas. An increasing number of craft dropped anchor off Sri Lanka's west coast near a rocky headland shown on Ptolemy's map of AD 154 as the "Cape of Jupiter" — one of the great landmarks for ancient navigators making their way south to the harbour of Galle. A settlement of "Moors" and Sinhalese lay between the headland called by them Ygandhara, and a small river, the Kalany, not far from the capital of a Sinhalese King of Kotte a few miles from the coast. The "Moors" eventually converted the name of the river and the settlement to Kalambu.

It was at Kalambu that a Portuguese, Dom Laurenco de Almeida, "discovered" Ceylon in 1501 — some say 1506 — on his way to confront a naval challenge to Portuguese power in India. How his brigantine happened to appear off Sri Lanka is not known, perhaps a whim of the monsoon. The ships' companies came ashore and de Almeida claimed the settlement for Portugal. They immediately changed its name to Colombo, pleased to find the old name so like the hero of the day, Christof Colombo. The Sinhalese were amazed at the strange beings in the streets, the first European fighting men ever seen. An old Sinhalese chronicle reports: "In Ceylon the people went about saying: There is in our harbour of Colombo a race of people fair of skin and comely withal. They don jackets of iron and hats of iron: they rest not a minute in one place: they walk here and there: they eat hunks of stone (bread) and drink blood (wine): and give two or three pieces of gold and silver for one fish or one lime: the report of their cannon is louder than thunder when it bursts upon the rock Ygandhara. Their cannonballs fly many a gawwa and shatter fortresses of granite."

Dom Laurenco's report reached Portugal and Rome in 1507 and was the talk of Europe. "...a great procession was organized...to celebrate the event...a lengthy oration in praise of the Pope, to whom (was) ascribed not a little of the glory of the "discovery". Twelve years later the Portuguese built a fortified trading settlement at Colombo, an event that "caused much astonishment to the natives and grief to the Moors..." The "Moors" had gone quietly about their enterprise for centuries saying little about the charms of their private paradise. Not Portugal! The trading nations, for the tempo of the time, acted swiftly. By the end of the century, 1595, Holland organised a "Company for Distant Lands" and sent a fleet of merchantmen to trade with the East. Their ships, following the Portuguese route, worked their way round the Cape of Good Hope, where the Flying Dutchman began his career, traded with Java and China, and in 1602 arrived at Sri Lanka, to the distress of the Portuguese who had engaged themselves pleasantly since 1518 in the lucrative spice trade and in converting the islanders to Christianity.

For fifty years the Dutch and the Portuguese fought for control of the coasts and the rich cinnamon plantations. They fought at the ports, through jungles and foothills. In 1650 Danish and English merchantmen moved into Sri Lankan waters stirring up a tumultuous row that delighted the King of the Sinhalese safe in his capital in the hills. He actively encouraged each of the rivals in a game of "a plague on all your houses" by secret treaties and alliances with each against the others; and he added a footnote for the French when they looked in briefly in 1664 hoping for trade. The King encouraged them too, but when the British challenged them, the French backed off.

The Dutch decided on a bold stroke and in 1658 mounted a six months' seige of Colombo that finally defeated the Portuguese. Of that last day of the seige, Joao Ribero, out of 400 men one of the few who survived, wrote in his memoirs: "By nine o'clock at night we had no more men to fight with them, and they had come and followed us into the street, without doubt they would easily have killed the few we had. That night they brought a quantity of fascones and earth with which they made parapets towards the city, and by morning they had turned the artillery: when we saw this, a Council was held to decide what should be done under the circumstances. Some voted for sending the few women and children we had into a church and setting it and the whole city on fire, while the few men who remained should die sword in hand in the midst of the enemy, so that the very memory of the people of this city might not be left, and the enemy might not boast of his conquest. The prelates of the religious orders who were present at this meeting vetoed the suggestion, declaring that such would be the work of gentiles and utter barbarians, and one condemned by all laws human and divine; our duty was to resign ourselves to the will of God and not to oppose His Divine decrees: for though the King of Portugal had laid special importance on the defence of the Island, yet it was his Ministers who would be called upon to explain why no relief was sent."

The Portuguese were the first builders of permanent houses in Sri Lanka, most of which the Dutch demolished. And although the Portuguese methods of religious conversion were often ruthless, many islanders became Christians. Their descendants make up a large minority. In 1540 Joao de Barros wrote: "The Portuguese arms and pillars placed in countless isles...are material things, and time may destroy them. But time will not destroy the religion, customs and language which the Portuguese have implanted in those lands."

Holland enjoyed an immensely profitable monopoly for 128 years; fortified Colombo harbour, dredged lakes and canals, laid out the streets of the city, built churches and pleasant villas. Although the British presence was everywhere in India and Asia, the Dutch refused British merchants trading rights on the island. But a stroke of British diplomatic genius brought off an international coup: Persuading the defeated ruler of Holland, Prince William of Orange, then exiled in England, to cede Dutch colonies to them, the British secretly bought off the European owners of the regiment of mercenaries hired by the Dutch to defend their Ceylonese ports. A message was rushed across a third of the globe by ship, camel and rowboat, carried by a secret courier to inform the Commander of the mercenaries of the sudden transfer of allegiance. The English fleet were discreetly out of sight, but the Dutch Governor at Colombo became suspicious and refused the Englishman all contact with the garrison. Quick thinking neutralized the Govenor; the message was smuggled to the Commander of the mercenaries in a Dutch cheese. As soon as the regiment sailed for India, the British attacked the undefended garrison and captured Ceylon in 1796 in an almost bloodless victory.

By 1880, years of peaceful management of the island brought sightseers. Moncure Daniel Conway sailed down from the north east past the dry north plains of Sri Lanka. "On a warm summer day in the middle of December voyaging on a sea of glass I beheld…a long white cloud low in the horizon. It was Ceylon – the land of my dreams." And dreams, psychologists say, the night dreams of sleep, are a hidden spur to adventure in all of us.

In the 1930's Eugene Wright couldn't resist the island. "…the mate had come aft and bawled out…No shore leave for *nobody*, and looked me squarely in the eye, I knew I would go ashore…Tall coconut palms, the tallest and most luxuriant I have ever seen, swayed gently over the white beach; little red tile roofs…fleets of strange craft, crazily shaped, gaudily painted…I slid down the rope ladder (and) in a half hour's time set foot on the island of Ceylon."

A hundred years ago, repairs on the Colombo breakwater turned up a black stone weighing 27 tons carved with the royal arms of Portugal and a date either 1501 or 1506 — it is quite worn. Old chronicles say Dom de Almeida set up a commemorative stone when he left Colombo. The stone stands now in a park of the President's Gardens. The carving is skilfully done. Gazing at the Royal Arms, we are flashed a vision of men in bright armour, gold-fringed crimson banners in the sun, cannons saluting the little settlement of huts as brigantines up-anchor and sail away, sails billowing; a vision as bizarre and fanciful as the Hindu myth of the Demon King of Lanka crossing the sea in his flying chariot. In the next 500 years of Sri Lanka's ocean history, will our big planes, and the tourists, seem as unimaginable?

1. Gadaladeniya Temple.

2. Buddha Image, Gadaladeniya.

3. Timber-roofed Dagoba, Gadaladeniya.

4. Lankatilaka Temple, Handessa.

5. Buddha Image, Lankatilaka.

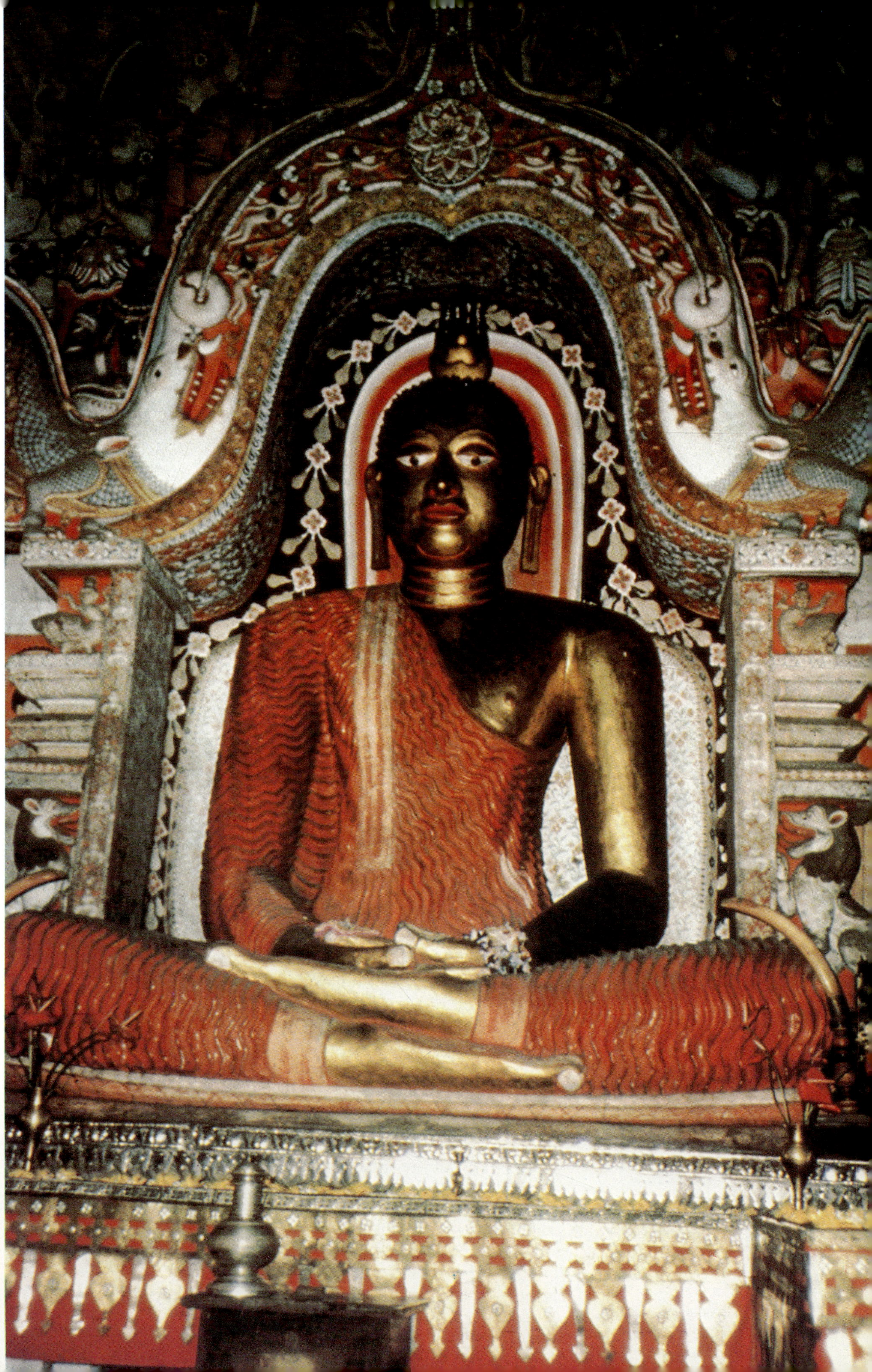

6. Entrance to Embekke Devale.

7. Roof ridge construction, Embekke Devale.

8. Eave construction, Embekke Devale.

9. Grain storage houses, Embekke.

10. Entrance pavilion, Alutnuwara.

11. A worshipper at Alutnuwara.

12. King of Kandy. Dodantale mural.

13. A farmer-musician. Near Dodantale.

14. Bridge at Bogoda Vihara.

15. Polk at the Bogoda Footbridge.

16 Temple porch, Badulla

CHAPTER II

CITIES OF THE OLD KINGDOM

"Colombo as a town presents little to attract a stranger", writes Emerson Tennant. "It possesses neither the romance of antiquity nor the interest of novelty...The locality presents no single advantage to recommend it." Perhaps an understatement...Colombo sprawls across the humid seafront without noticeable charm. The Fort is a contrived harbour and its backdrop of buildings all business; there is the sea fenced off; side streets of fine big trees and colonial houses...But there are the enormous crowds of an overgrown, unplanned, untidy tropical city. Compensations can be found: living permanently in Colombo in secluded compounds with friends nearby is a choice made by many people from the western nations. But in the short term...

Miseries of Colombo, 1859: "The nightly serenade of frogs (some of which are of gigantic dimensions), the tormenting profusion of mosquitoes, and the incredible swarms of more ignoble flies, cause a nuisance sometimes intolerable. So multitudinous are these insects at certain seasons, that...flies invade the apartments in such numbers as literally to extinguish the lights..." (Sir James Emerson Tennant).

Miseries of Colombo, 1980: The slick big hotel air conditioning is so cold we can't sleep; the windows cannot be opened. We move to a flat in an elegant house in a tree shaded street. No air conditioning, no glass in the windows — the natural life, the real Sri Lanka...the real enormous spiders, the real ant swarms, and flies, and sweat on the brow, and damp clothes, and packs of street curs barking and fighting all night, and mosquitoes, several under the nets with us where there's no air, and the "no-see-ums" that have colonized the cane furniture and nip through thin clothes. After a week we drove south for a few days at Galle.

The road to Galle, 1859: "In its peculiar style of beauty, nothing in the world can exceed in loveliness the road from Point de Galle to Colombo; it is literally an avenue of palms, nearly seventy miles long, with a rich under-growth of tropical trees, many crimson flowers...orchids,...climbing plants. Birds of gaudy plumage dart amidst the branches, gay butterflies hover...insects of metallic lustre glitter on the leaves...Where a view of the landscape can be caught...it is equally grand and impressive on every side...the range of purple hills...the blue sea, studded with rocky inlets...The beach carpeted with verdure...in the shade of....luxuriant groves nestle the white cottages of the natives...some...on the model of old Dutch villas..." (Emerson Tennant).

Lovely is the word, lovely to see, but the underlying silence of the 19th century is gone, and the pleasant beat of horse hooves marking the rhythm of the day's drive. Our car growls down the middle of the road on a collision course. There is dust on the leaves, rubbish on the edge of the road, a smell of petrol and exhaust fumes. The grass huts are still there, and the little Dutch villas. Tappers are high in the toddy palms; ropes stretched between trees are tight-ropes, the men walk them fast balancing their buckets. Beyond the 20th century blight are still the deep groves where the loveliness survives. We drive a quarter mile on a side road. "Dear me, it is beautiful—and most sumptuously tropical in the character of foliage and the opulence of it...whole libraries of sentiment and oriental charm and mystery and tropic deliciousness." But Mark Twain was wicked enough to add that the palms looked like feather dusters struck by lightning.

Galle, once a charming town built by the Dutch, is in decline; the beautiful harbour between fortified rocky headlands has little business. The huge old hotel is a proud and ponderous wood panelled, overstuffed, velour draped, mouldy threadbare relic. Our room was the size of a double garage, the ceiling up high in the gloom. Afloat in the room stood two vast four poster beds fitted with heavy, dark carved wood canopies from which fell aged panels of red velvet and knots of grubby mosquito net. We backed out of the room, paid for the unspent night, and found a bright little motel-like hostelry on a rock cliff over the sea not romantic, but clean, fresh, breeze-swept — the ocean breaking below.

Emerson Tennant has the last word on Galle: "Galle is by far the most venerable emporium of foreign trade, now existing in the universe; it was the resort of merchant ships at the earliest dawn of commerce, and it is destined to be the centre to which will hereafter converge all the rays of navigation, intersecting the Indian Ocean, and connecting the races of Europe and Asia." But "hereafter" is a long time, and, who knows? Perhaps the genius of science fiction will devise a floating sky port over the harbour of Galle?

Colombo is on the western edge of the influence of the rainy mountains, and for forty miles north along the coast past canals, villages and old Portuguese churches, a cover of magnificent trees arches over the road, gardens and houses. Colours flair in the shadows: a man in a purple shirt and peacock blue sarong flashes along on his bicycle, a girl in a flame red saree carries a yellow sunshade. In the dim green air, flowers, birds and people look like jewels.

We took a side road to the beach, to a sandspit where villagers had gathered. Fishermen were hauling a boat on to the sand, coming in with the morning's catch – they go out long before dawn and return mid morning. The men heaved and tugged at the boat; people leaned over the side, pointing, arguing, choosing fish. A fisherman left the crowd and walked toward the road, his fingers hooked under the gills of two coral-pink fish, magnificent, long nosed creatures, slender and shapely as Celini bronzes, and so big their tails dragged in the sand although the man was tall. His build was a *prime danseur's*, he was remarkably handsome and his eyes glistened with the excitement of his fine catch. We called a compliment and he held up a fish for us to admire.

The island's climates follow the ups and downs of the shape of the land: the low northern plains are the dry tropics, hot and arid; the wet tropics are in the south under the mountains — 6,000 feet of rain-catching, forest-garbed, geological terraces. Along the mountain valleys, rivers and streams fall in wide loops and winding confluences that from the air might look like silver threads tossed from a rolling spool. The mountains influence about a third of the island, and the climate changes as abruptly as the island's silhouette.

We decided to drive north. At the half-way point of the coast and in the spell of the arid plains is Puttalam, a town on a famous harbour where about BC 500 the first Aryans disembarked to found the ancient kingdom of Sinhala. We disembarked for lunch at a small public restaurant, the only place within miles to eat. Tour buses and cars crammed the inadequate courtyard; we should have been braced for what we found. The tourist onslaught had demoralized the place. They coped as they could. We made our getaway. At least Puttalam at that time broke the monotony of the near perfection of paradise island. The sea offers the beach a cool moist layer of air, but the road turns east rising on to the plains. Within a half mile of the up-turn, cool moist air becomes hot moist air that soon dehydrates to hot dry air, a sharp change triggering a refrigerator effect as sweat evaporated from our clothes. Shivering in the heat we reached for cardigans — a mere 400 miles from the Equator. We learned to keep them within reach.

The sky changed, too. Near the coast the sea is a rippled mirror reflecting sunlight in shimmers against salt mists stored in the air. This double play of rays lays a sea-light over the colour of the sky. But on the inland plain sunlight streams down unfiltered, and the sky is a clean limitless blue. The sky expands and we look into space. The intense blue of this window on the universe is set off by semi-arid landswells bleached pale buff and lying in rounded, almost human contours over outcrops of the island's dark, smooth volcanic bed-rock.

We came to a shallow valley where a covering of shrubby trees was pierced by many big boulders — wild elephant country. "Last week I was driving people here, and around this turn..." The driver slowed to a crawl and we held our breath. But no elephant. It was just as well, lone males are dangerous. Alexander's admiral wrote in his report in BC 323: "The elephants bred in the island are bigger and more fierce and furious for war service than those of India." Elephants trained for war were one of the commodities Sri Lanka exported to the ancient Mediterranean.

A big one stood in the road the week before and the driver slammed on his brakes waiting for the animal to choose a direction; he strolled into the valley. "What would you have done?" "Turn around and try to outrun him. There's a hill back there, elephants can't run down hill." A number of cars were parked along the road. "Tourists looking for elephants." We drove slowly easily imagining the big brown rocks tc be browsing elephants. We crested the end of the valley. Rolling towards us..."Work elephant." The two words made a world of difference. Green branches bristling from the sides of his trunk and obscuring the mahout walking chain in hand were his midday rations; work elephants carry their food to work, their favourite is a sweet-sapped tree, the Tika tree. Elephants tell the time by the feel of the sun and at mid-day stop work and expect to eat, and stories go round that sometimes an elephant will put down his mahout with a heavy foot if the greens don't come on fast enough.

The work-elephant was a handsome beast striding with an air of benign condescension. The trainable Asian race have been part of human history. Their great strength and intelligence make them useful in dense jungle, but their enormous appetite requiring unlimited trees and shrubs, their need for water, and, strangely, their delicate constitution, limit their range, and modern Sri Lanka may not support herds of wild elephant for long. Jungles are being cleared for people and the famous game reserves are too small for more than a few. Elephants need jungle room; they are shy and like to be alone, loving solitude so much that intrusions alarm them, even a rabbit starting from the brush. They are so sensitive they can die of loneliness and chagrin; soon after being captured and the first rage and resistance is spent, an elephant may suddenly lie down and die — the people say of a broken heart. Once one is tamed his intelligence is striking; he seems to understand his job and takes the initiative to improve his performance. He will size up a job, judging the weight to be tackled against his strength, and if he is urged on against his judgement he may become angry. So many elephants have been killed for ivory that Sri Lanka bans ivory carving except with African tusks. Sri Lankan elephants will soon be "an endangered species".

We drove toward the north east with our solemn driver, at a pace of regal dignity. The old land showed its age. October had seared the hills, the rocks were filmed over with heat-dust, the trees were listless. The monsoon rains, a miraculous fountain of youth that rejuvenates the highlands to the south, simply deepens the erosions of the plains.

In 1813 Samuel Newell made this trip. "Most of the way is either barren heath or a desert, filled with wild elephants, wild hogs, bears and tigers. Travellers are obliged to carry all their provisions with them, even their own water. My train consisted of 14 persons — 12 for my palanquin and two for my baggage. I travelled in the night, as is usual on account of the heat of the day, when you are obliged to rest. My bearers carried torches (note: these would be flaming oil-soaked cloth on poles) and kept up a great noise to keep off the wild beasts...It will excite surprise...to hear of travelling in this manner. There is no other way...no stages, no private carriages, no horses to be had...on account of the badness of the roads and the weakness of the horses. Walking in this country is extremely dangerous." Newell was seven days on a journey that took us a few hours.

A monotony like waking sleep...A quiet settled in us, a gift from the somnolent land preparing us for the ancient kingdoms, for a "journeying in the flesh (that becomes) an adventure of the mind". The car circled a knoll and we entered a long wide valley flanked by ranges of rounded hills. On crests a mile or so apart stood three immense white comical structures as arresting, as heart-stopping, as space ships from another galaxy.

"Ancient dagobas", said the driver. We were approaching Anuradhapura.

Prehistory

The earliest people, moving out to populate the earth from a probable evolutionary source of humanity in south central Asia, arrived in India between glacial ages. When the last epoch began those who did not enjoy a life like that lived until recently by Eskimos drifted south as the ice came down, and crossed into Sri Lanka. A tribe of primitive people live still in the island forests — the Vedda, called the "wild men" by the Sinhalese. The Veddas carry on a hunter-gatherer way of life and practise an archaic method of barter: one will lay an object for barter on the ground, then hide in the brush; another emerges, and, if he likes it, picks it up and puts down his trade object and disappears. The first man claims his new object and the deal is closed…no word spoken, no argument — it is called "silent barter" and comes from so remote a time that language may not have been known. The Veddas of Sri Lanka fight off the inroads of civilization. They may be a remnant people like the Gonds of India, of comparatively pure neolithic stock.

In the age of India's great legend Rama and Sita languished in the Vindhya Hills, and Ravana, the dashing ten-headed Demon King of Lanka enticed Sita into his Flying Chariot. Under the aerial surveillance of the Eagle King and marshalled by Hanuman, King of the Monkeys, the animal kingdoms built a land bridge to rescue Sita. "While the bridge was being built the deafening noises produced by the mallets, and the incessant cries of "Victory to Rama" rent the air…When the bridge extended to 160 miles in length, hundreds of squirrels came to the sea-shore to assist in the work…they rolled their bodies among heaps of dust (on the shore), then, going up to the bridge, they shook off the dust, and thus effectually filled the minute crevices" (Calcutta Review, No. X, translation of the Ramayana [c. 1850]). The facts underlying the legend begin perhaps with the emerging land bridge 10,000 years ago, and consequent tribal struggles with seven tribes of Sri Lanka…art recording life.

Then the fair tawny haired Aryans appear as heroic and poetic, Homeric, a people alive to the rhythms of action. Before the development of writing, a body of literature and tribal law had been preserved in detail by the priests, men whose lives were to embody the whole of tribal memory — the history, laws, cautionary tales, poetry, intricate theological and philosophical speculations. Learned by rote from boyhood, they passed down over a hundred generations the lore of the ancients, retained in such exactness that when the craft of writing evolved priests separated in time and place wrote them out in almost identical terms.

The Aryan conquerors reduced the people of the land, called the Deshi, to servile roles that could not be included in the four long established divisions necessary to the prosperity of the tribe: the priests — rememberers of knowledge; the defenders — kings and warriors; businessmen — traders and suppliers; and husbandmen. They took a different view of the lords of the Indian animal kingdom, Siva's great lions, then a remnant now reduced to a handful. The Aryans saw the lion as the counterpart of themselves, warrior nobles, and immediately called themselves the Sinhala, Lion People, a name, a footnote from prehistory, still alive in the names Singh, Sinha, and the Sinhalese. Indra, their dominant god, has that honour too; their name for lion, Sinha, may possibly ring a peal for Indra, and the river, Indus, and the land, Sind, and the nation India.

The migrations of the Aryans into India covered centuries. Each tribal chief, as the tribe emerged on the plains, turned his people to explore east, or south-east or south. The Sakya tribe a people of the Gautama clan set up a prospering kingdom about BC 800 in the Himalayan foothills. In BC 563 a son was born to their king who named him Siddhartha; 35 years later as the Buddha his influence would transform much of the Asian world.

About the time of Siddhartha's birth a wayward son of the king of the Sinhala tribe set out from the north west with a company of friends to fight their way south to the tip of India. There they asked about the island on the horizon, heard the superlatives, requisitioned boats, sailed over and claimed it, calling it Sinhala. Vijaya, as their king, included scattered colonies of the earlier settlers as a *de facto* kingdom and gave his clan's name to them all — they became the Sinhalese. His was the first Sinhalese dynasty of Sri Lanka...Much of the story is legend, but a respected one and carried down by the priesthood in the ancient way. That the early Sinhalas engineered the first irrigation system, about BC 400 is an accepted fact; they began the canal-linked lake-reservoir planning that supported a rich civilization for 2,000 years; a system so technically excellent that modern hydrologists consider it superior to Roman aqueduct building. The Sinhalese spread water systematically across almost level land.

Throughout all these earliest centuries kingdoms depended on the fertility of the fields and this depended on water supply, and, in the north, on this intricate network of irrigation. There was nothing like it in India and the warlike South Indians were attracted to the rich rice fields of the north of the island. There is high praise due for the science and skill shown in these extensive irrigation works still very much in evidence today and partly still in use. It is not known how the engineers and technicians set about their work or what instruments they used. The fall in the ancient canals was from 1 foot to 6 inches per mile.

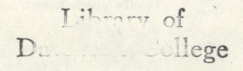

Anuradhapura

Two events of the 6th century BC (the birth of Siddhartha, the Buddha, and Vijaya's arrival on Sri Lanka) are believed by Buddhists to be miraculously related; and also the founding of the capital, Anuradhapura about BC 320 by Vijaya III, who may have been a descendant of Vijaya I. The king hearing of the grandeur of the Maurya Empire of North India built his magnificent capital, and named it for a sacred constellation of stars, Anuradha. Seventy-five years later came another step in the predestined purpose: Asoka, Emperor of India and a convert to Buddhism, sent a mission to Sri Lanka led by his son Mahinda, and his daughter Sangamitta who brought with her a portentous gift for the Sinhalese king — a sapling from the sacred Bo-tree under which Siddhartha on that night of the full moon found Enlightenment and became the Buddha, the Enlightened One. In the centuries after the arrival of the sapling the dynasty founded by Vijaya fulfilled its unique purpose: to provide a world sanctuary for the Buddha's teaching.

The Bo-tree of Anuradhapura: an explosion of leaves flares behind high walls; beyond an ornate gateway, a massive, tangled tree, entwined upon itself, is engaged in a millennial struggle to survive another 2000 years. The account of its age is believable. Silent people sit separately in the expanse of its shadow. A whisper from the sea of leaves and countless tiny banners quiver in the dry morning air — the only sound. The battered, propped up tree is watched day and night by men, hereditary guards, who are believed to be descended from the protectors of the little sapling. The King, Devanampiya Tissa, planted the tree himself and ordered an aqueduct built to water it. In AD 411 the Chinese pilgrim scholar, Fa-Hsien, saw the tree. "As this tree bent over toward the south-east the king feared it would fall, and therefore placed props at eight or nine spans at the circumference to support it." The tree caused concern 1300 years later following 600 years of neglect; King Kirti Sri Rajasinha of Kandy ordered the present formidable stone wall built to keep off the wild elephants.

Fa-Hsien, a young Buddhist scholar, determined to find and copy texts of the Buddha's teaching unknown in China, set out from Ch'ang-an on foot, travelling through the Gobi desert with only the bones of the dead to guide him. He made a perilous descent through the Hindu Kush and came to India. Then after 3 years he voyaged to Sri Lanka where he spent two years copying the ancient manuscripts. Returning to China after 15 years with his precious copies, the merchant ship ran into a heavy gale; all bulky goods were thrown

17. Exterior murals, Badulla.

18. Detail of Badulla mural.

19. Detail of Badulla mural.

20. The high sanctuary roofs, Ratnapura Devale.

21. Demon mural, Ratnapura.

22. The verandah banquet table, Ekneligoda.

23. The Medawala Vihara.

24. Anuradha Seneviratna (left) at the Monk's house, Ridi Vihara.

overboard, but Fa-Hsien managed to save his manuscripts although the Hindu sailors threatened to throw over both him and the papers after him, but he continued praying to "the Hearer of Prayers" saying "I have journeyed on behalf of the Faith. So that by your awful power you would grant me a safe return." He lived to be 88, and wrote his splendid memoirs on bamboo tablets and silk, an account of what he had been through.

Describing his experiences in Sri Lanka Fa-Hsien speaks of one of Buddhism's most venerated reminders of the man who became the Buddha: the sacred Tooth Relic. He tells about a public viewing of the Tooth: "...a man who speaks well, dressed in royal robes and mounted on a caparisoned elephant, announced the event thus: "Let all those ecclesiastics and laymen...who wish to lay up happiness for themselves, help to level roads, decorate the streets and prepare flowers, incense and implements of worship." The Sacred Tooth is then brought out and passes along the central streets, receiving the homage of offerings as it goes by..."

The saga of the Sacred Tooth is an amalgam of fact and fiction. Eight hundred years after the Buddha died in BC 483 the Tooth surfaced in Anuradhapura. Apparently the Relic had been secreted in Kalinga, east India, and now the King feared that Hindu fanatics in a time of Brahmanic resurgence would discover his dynastic treasure, arranged for his daughter, Princess Hemamala, to visit Lanka. His pious strategy was this: hidden in the hair of the Princess Royal was the Relic. Hemamala presented it to King Sri Meghavarna. The princess smuggled the Tooth to Sri Lanka about AD 313; a pillared hall was built that enshrined the Tooth during those centuries of the Anuradhapura kings.

Fa-Hsien describes the great city: "the Abhayagiri Dagoba and the monastery where there are now five thousand monks. There is in it a hall of the Buddha, adorned with carved and inlaid work of gold and silver, and rich in the seven precious substances...an image (of the Buddha) in green jade more than twenty cubits high...the dwellings of the merchants are very grand; and the side streets and main thoroughfares are level and well-kept...where four roads meet...are chapels for preaching the Faith...a lofty dias is arranged where ecclesiastics and laymen come...to hear the Faith expounded...The King (endowing a temple) provided a golden plough (with) fine oxen with horns richly decorated with gold, silver, and other valuables...with his own hands he ploughed round the four sides of (the) piece of ground...and ceded to the priesthood, population, fields, houses and all (for) generation to generation..."

1823. The Collector's Office at Mannar. Mannar is the long sand-spit island and gulf famous for pearls to the ancients, and for the dugongs, fishlike mammals with round heads and silky hair that inspired the tales of mermaids told by Greek sailors of antiquity. And there were other rumours: ruins in the deep forest on the mainland; man-made hills hundreds of feet high stand in dense jungle; a hill of a thousand steps; caves, figures made of a stone so transparent they shine like lights; a hill carved into a colossus; circles of columns in the impenetrable brush. Thomas Ralph Blackhouse, British Collector of Mannar, listened to the rumours brought by his men and listened himself to the country people. There were no roads, but his intelligent curiosity put him on watch. Forcing his way on horseback into the rank malarial groves he found a few scattered families, a wretched, disease ridden, dying population, and he found the stones of a great lost city, Anuradhapura, long drowned in jungle, and vanished from official history. The British government, not then particularly interested in the ruins, were very interested in reports of huge dry or stagnant reservoirs and channels, and in the desperate people. Roads were begun, a programme for restoring the tanks and channels was pioneered which, within decades, pressed the jungles back to provide farmland, and there was much less malaria. By 1850 pious Buddhists came on pilgrimage to the sacred places now visible in the forests; they helped to clear jungle trees from the ruins. With the practical work going well, the government turned its attention to history. H.C.P. Bell, an archaeologist, was appointed to undertake the unearthing of Sri Lanka's forgotten cities.

1980. A guest house at Anuradhapura. We have read the memoirs and romantic histories. The car glides down the drive through the green lawns of the guest house at Anuradhapura and out the gate. We came after dark and saw nothing of the landscape. Now we see that everything beyond the garden gate is the colour of a desert winter — grey-brown. Tree leaves, tree trunks, road, rocks — all bleached by October to the dullness of deserts. We look about expecting splendours...we drive on past spindly groves and waste places. The car stops and we look about; several dozen plain thin pillars of rough stone lean among a few thin trees. "The famous Brazen Palace", explains the driver. "But where is Anuradhapura?" "Here, all round here. All this is Anuradhapura!" The driver stretches his arm toward the dust-dull landscape. Ahead we see a big mound where people are clambering about it, climbing on a bamboo scaffolding, laying a skin of bricks over the mound. "Ancient dagoba repair", explains the driver. We drive on; another dagoba...By now some of the disappointment has worn away, and the feeling of unease, as if some marvel is all about us that we cannot see. Garden cities are splendid when alive, but dead, a garden city is a smattering of memories. The huge mound before us was a memory.

We studied it. Extraordinary! 400 feet high and once sheathed with brick, and a facing of white 'stucco' ("The preparation consists of lime, coconut water and the glutinous juice of a fruit which grows upon the paragaha-tree") and topped with a gilded spire. And at the centre, the very inner point of the great bulk was one hair, a forehead hair, of the Buddha.

Could we imagine reading a cosmic significance into every object or place, each minute activity of the day let alone the events and thrusts of nations? The dagobas, a form of the universal egg, half seen, half unseen; at the fertile centre, equally pressing with its infinite power on all the dimensions of being, is the point — the *dot* — through which the psyche enters *Nirvana*...the infinitely expanding sphere of all knowing and no knowing; a point, an instant, similar to modern physics' theories of numberless dimensions entered at intersections, "warps" with other kinds of universes...the "psychic shift".

By the end of the day we had made discoveries that compensated for the undiscoverable city: the museum's collection of superb bronzes; the foundations and columns once the shrine of the Sacred Tooth; a bathing pool finely designed, brilliantly made. In a sacred grove of the 7th century a rounded rock hillock with a lotus pond at its base had been sculpted in the shape of two elephants sporting in the water. A guide crept along a ledge, splashed the rock so the flanks of the carved elephants glistened like wet hide. Returning in late afternoon we saw a stone figure sitting on a high plinth under a canopy. We looked at it a long time. The figure was plain — once it had been jewelled and sat beside the Bo-tree. Now on the dusty roadside the image, face and posture, pours out celestial wisdom as purely as a human body can.

We had seen the model of a roofed dagoba in the museum, a roof over one of these huge dagobas. The archaeologist Bell believed they had been roofed, and the profession has puzzled about it ever since. An intriguing idea, but wood tends to be straight and fitting a wood roof on a dome would be complex. Were they in fact roofed? Could the question be answered by ancient building traditions that still exist? When we got to the hills this question sharpened our eyes.

The December monsoon of the east coast has less rain than the summer deluge in the west, and the landscape around Trincomalee has a dry, wistful appearance. The high ground is sparsely covered but dips and valleys have grown up with delicate woodlands. The old town edges the north side of the harbour and a Portuguese fort on a headland overlooks the immense bay almost circular and about nine miles across, a dramatic sight recently marred by a utilitarian factory on the far side that dwarfs the hills.

In the tussles between trading nations of the 17th century, the Sinhalese King Senarat ceded the port to the Danes in a fruitless effort to outflank the Portuguese. A Danish priest wrote: "one can smell the romantic scents of Ceylon at a distance of 16 miles over the sea."

Under the British the bay became an important naval base. William Pitt declared to parliament: Trincomalee "(is) to us the most valuable Colonial possession on the globe...the finest and most advantageous Bay in the whole of India...the equal of which is hardly known, in which a whole fleet may safely ride and remain in tranquillity." It is still true.

Emily and I skirted the town, turned north, and the port buildings vanished behind the smooth hills. A lagoon lay to the left flanked by reeds. We were on the peninsula called Nilaveli. "The big hotel is arranged for you", the driver announced. "No. We'll stay in a small hotel." The car slowed while he looked round as if seeing us for the first time. "Ah, yes...atmosphere. Another five miles."

The Anuradhapura guest house had been an English country house with wide balconies and white shutters in acres of garden. At breakfast we had been invited to the kitchens to see them cook our 'hoppers', a thin crisp *crepe* made from rice flour and coconut milk, a mixture looking rather like the recipe for the plaster on dagobas, but without the lime and paragaha fruit. A sub-cook, neat and sweating creamed milk from the coconut, pressing it onto a round-headed, hand-cranked drill fastened to the wall. In another room individual iron bowls smoked over gas jets. A ladle of hopper mix went into four bowls, and the chef seized each in turn swirling the batter up round the sides; eggs dropped in the centres cooked through in a flash and the hopper edges curled over making a nest of golden brown flounces.

We were not going to settle for one of Trincomalee's air conditioned hotels after that.

The peninsula is flat and the road merely a deep rut between brambles and scrub trees higher than the road. The road had been fairly wide at first but narrowed to a single track. The sea light and dry air made us squint. The driver looked round. "Last hotel, you will like this one." In the front of the house the garden was an acre of shapely trees trimmed to become an interlocking sunfilter over lawns and flower borders. On a terrace people sat comfortably at tables. Down a path toward the sea were a group of cabins that could have come from Japan: weathered wood, pitched roofs under fine trees. We smiled at the driver. "Very nice. We do like it."

Three walls of our cabin were simply rows of narrow wooden louvres, a pull and a thrust slanted them ajar. Set into each wall of louvres were large windows held open by wood slats hinged inside. Our north window opened on the lagoon. Trees shadowed the water starred with lotuses and riffled by waterbirds. On the east we glimpsed the blue sea through a screen of trees edged by yellow sand. The south window faced the lawn. Eight or nine handsome ponies grazed there looking in the green light like intaglios carved in green glass. Mosquito nets hung over the beds. We had tucked in for a doze when the creak of a branch nearby woke us. A troup of monkeys crouched in the trees and clearly heading for our cabin were watching an old female on the ground. Her head craned round, she advanced, the troup swung forward above her. They were less than 15 feet away and a dash would do it. Our hands were on the window braces when we heard the wise one give a hoot and saw her jump for a tree. Down the lane trotted three sleek dogs led by a matronly bitch. The team sauntered to the monkey tree, circled it at a slow trot, the queen-dog looking up. In one wild burst the monkeys swung off branch to branch toward a far edge of the garden. While the dogs watched them go, the queen strolled to an arbour nearby, mounted a slanted slab to a pedestal and surveying the ground sniffed for messages. They were·the shepherds of the monkeys, the waiter, Tamby, told us. She trained each litter. Monkey dogs were in demand in Trincomalee.

Tamby, the waiter who chose to take care of us, was a small ex-sailor who had seen it all. Thirty years in the British navy, tattooed to the point of no return, Tamby was convinced that Ladies made the decisions and studiously avoided consulting the Masters. "What will the Master like for tiffin, Lady?" he'd ask at breakfast. Tamby took small advantages if we were friendly; if we were firm he sulked: the world-wide response to a surfeit of tourists.

Polonnaruwa

The driver leaned on the car waiting for us to satisfy our incomprehensible interest in a flock of ordinary birds. We were on our way to Polonnaruwa having shaken off the lassitude of the lagoon. We'd watched lizards skitter on the dry road and now saw strange birds walking on pools that were more weed than water, pools that possibly were part of the ancient water system. We stopped the driver at his full thrust of 25 mph for a look at the bizarre birds. They were manoeuvring on splayed feet with long toes thin as grass stems — a technical innovation evolved over how many millennia so that large black and white jacana could catch water insects — the birds were one more minute link in the vast creation tailored for a tiny destiny. We returned to the car where the driver stood patiently resigned to our whims. William Hull spelled out the expression on the driver's face..."Everybody talks about the physical beauty and grace of the Ceylonese, the dignity of the saronged villager and the loin-clothed farmer, the courtesy, the spontaneous hospitality, the inbred politeness. But one phase of that politeness needs emphasis: the gentle tolerance of the eccentricities of foreigners, the immediate masking of that little light in the eye that reflects speculations about basic sanity."

We were subdued and our thoughts on the dead-end destinies of birds drifted to the fate of nations. The driver tried to cheer us up. "Very old land with much trouble", he said. We knew the history. What would one of the inheritors say..."What happened to this land?"

"Fever and fighting. Many long years of fighting and fever killed this land." Fever and fighting...in a nutshell.

Sri Lanka's people led an idyllic existence until the 5th century; their ancestors had come from many nations: Persia, Greece, Arabia, China and all parts of India but they were Sinhalese now, and the religions brought by their forebears were practised side by side. Fa-Hsien tells of listening to a Brahmin priest who inspired this devout Buddhist. Persians, Christians and Greeks traded with Arabs and South Indians. For reasons mixed as motives often are the South Indian Dravidian dynasty began a programme of expansion. The noble families had intermarried with the Sinhalese. The trade was immensely profitable, the gems, especially the pearls of Mannar, and the gold...their people were crowded on the land and Sri Lanka had land to spare. A simple matter of conquest, and the first steps would be gradual. Small invasion forces attacked Anuradhapura and were fought off; at least they retreated to the north tip of the island where many South Indians had settled in ancient times. By degrees, the invasions were strengthened, and saboteurs sent into the island to begin, behind the Sri Lankan forces, the breaking of units of the irrigation system. In the 6th century the mutual tolerance existing from the beginning disintegrated, and to the pressures of defending themselves were added conflicts along religious lines. The long term plan of conquest was paying off. Inter-island conflicts were doing the invader's work, and in the 11th century the unified ancient kingdoms called Pihiti of north Sri Lanka had broken into small warring kingdoms ripe for a full fledged invasion from South India. The strength of the attackers overwhelmed Anuradhapura. The city fell, the Sinhalese retreated toward the southern hills, and after 1300 years the lion and the lizard kept the courts of Anuradhapura. The city itself was not the goal of the South Indians. The goal was the annexation of Sri Lanka to the Tamil Kingdom. Farmers and small merchants from South India crossed in increasing numbers and settled on the north coast. The Tamil Cola kings were half way to their aim. But a powerful king appeared among the Sinhalese, Vijayabahu I, who rallied his people and began a long war of liberation expelling the invaders from the central plains and restoring a Sinhalese dynasty to rule the Sinhalese. Immediately the rivalries began again among the princes with claims to the kingship; but among them was a prince of outstanding authority who brought order to the ruling house, becoming Parakramabahu I. His programme of reconstruction brought Sri Lanka to the high point of the Old Kingdoms. He planned a new city south of Anuradhapura on the site of a summer palace that, although farther from the invaders' base, had also been sacked. The new capital would be a compact defendable city near the great river of Sri Lanka, the Mahaveli Ganga. The city was planned to stand beside an inland sea constructed by the hands of thousands of people under innovative engineers who devised a method of stone sluice valves to regulate the water level. The city grew into a magnificent walled capital of palaces, shrines, temples and the inland sea eventually covered 6,000 acres. The embankments of the Sea of Parakrama were planted with trees and flowering shrubs. Against the walls of the city, suburbs were built to house the population, and make their defence sure.

The Sinhalese enjoyed a prosperity never before seen on the island, a splendid fever of building expeditions. The expanded water system increased crops; the arts of the Sinhalese reached new heights. Yet within 200 years the city was deserted, and the Sinhalese had fled to the southern mountains.

The South Indians, consolidated in the north, shaped strategies for the final show-down and conquest of the island of Sri Lanka. But force was not their only weapon; they utilised the classic manoeuvre of conquest: the systematic destruction of the technological nerves of a target nation; in Sri Lanka the continuous disruption of the water-flow units, the intricate irrigation system on which the capital and the economy of the Sinhalese kingdom depended. To the surreptitious destruction of the canals and tanks by the invaders was added an inbuilt bonus: the farmers and engineers were drawn away from their work of maintenance and repair of the system to defend the city and spills of water stood by the channels and water courses.

Administrative records from the early centuries of Anuradhapura report outbreaks of a wasting fever. But the people lived in scattered farm villages or suburbs and the incidence of the fever had little effect on large affairs. Modern medical analysts conclude that even then in Sri Lanka the malaria mosquito bred during the dry season in pools left in stream beds and overflows of standing water.

The changed elements in malaria's impact on the Old Kingdoms came with the planning of Polonnaruwa. The new capital was compact for defence; with increased prosperity the increased population was housed in urban suburbs. The neglect and continued assaults on the irrigation system left large tracts of water after floods. The malaria mosquito flourished and carried fever to the suburban people. Malaria was the final blow.

By 1400 the Sinhalese retreated into the foothills, and from there began 200 years of effort to dislodge the South Indians who were now in control of two-thirds of the island. Can it be surmised that the surprise arrival of the Portuguese in 1501 was a mixed blessing that prevented Sri Lanka from finally becoming an Indian province, and thus preserved its role as a major sanctuary of Buddhism?

A young British soldier, Lieutenant Fagan, "discovered" the ruins of Polonnaruwa in 1820. The land had reverted to tropical forest but the importance of the stone city sent archaeologists on risky ventures to get to them. Expeditions were not possible without a strong company of guards and government aid; the forests were almost impassable, there were no bridges over the rivers and streams, the primitive forest tribes made trouble...and there was malaria. In the 1870's the British began the clearing of the forests to restore the ancient irrigation channels and the village tanks. Two main roads traversing the island improved conditions rapidly; the fever abated, and those few farmers who had stayed through the thin centuries began to prosper.

A travelling journalist, Maturin Murray Ballou, got to Polonnaruwa in 1882. "Here and there labyrinths of unexplored ruins are entirely hidden by lofty, broad-limbed trees and a tangle of low, dense shrub...We pause, and gaze thoughtfully at the desolation...It is not to be wondered at that learned...antiquarians make pilgrimages hither to see with their own eyes...these black-letter records of by-gone ages."

The ruins now stand clear and beautiful. Are they more beautiful with so much left to the imagination than when in full flower? "...Polonnaruwa is exquisite and the quiet it immediately imposes is deeply religious...All voices are hushed in the Wata-dage, one of the finest temples, even in ruins, and the finer for being lyric...the Wata-dage is warm as well as still and nobody can enter Lankatilleka with erect spirit. Nor chatter at Gal-Vihare. This group, magnificent in concept and loving in execution, contains what the world reveres in Buddhism." Thus, the effusive William Hull, academician.

Here is the mystic, Thomas Merton, on Polonnaruwa and the Gal-Vihare six days before his accidental death in Bangkok. "Polonnaruwa was such an experience that I could not write hastily of it...its vast area under trees. Fences. Few people. A dirt road. Lost. Then we find Gal Vihara...The path dips down to a wide, quiet hollow surrounded with trees. A low outcrop of rock, with a cave cut into it, and beside the cave a big seated Buddha on the left, a reclining Buddha on the right, an Ananda, I guess, standing by the head of the reclining Buddha. In the cave another seated Buddha...I am able to approach the Buddhas barefoot and undisturbed, my feet in wet grass, wet sand. Then the silence of the extraordinary face. The great smiles. Huge and yet subtle. Filled with every possibility, questioning nothing, knowing everything, rejecting nothing...*without refutation*, without some other argument...I was knocked over with relief and thankfulness at the *obvious* clarity of the figures...Looking at these figures I was suddenly almost forcibly jerked clean out of the habitual, half-tied vision of things, and an inner clearness, clarity, as if exploding from the rocks themselves, became evident and obvious...there is no puzzle, no problem, and really no 'mystery'...All problems are resolved and everything is clear, simple because what matters is clear...Surely...my Asian pilgrimage has come clear and purified itself...I know and have seen what I was obviously looking for. I don't know what else remains but I have now got beyond the shadow and the disguise..." Whatever one feels about the meaning and message of this early Buddhist work, its grandeur cannot be denied.

CHAPTER III

THE KANDY FORTRESS

On the way to Kandy — 1890: "The scenery grows wilder, of deeper tints, and more richly tropical. The surprises intoxicate and bewilder. Great boulders...and hills which grow into mountains different...from those in any other land...A great jagged rock, scarred and gashed by the storm and shock of ages...vines climb its rugged points...with their delicate, dallying fingers...Palms everywhere...climbing this wonderful hill...(there is no) release from the sweet bondage of this perfumed and dazzling scene — ...new and strangely fascinating (in) lawlessness of colour. Nature's extravagant display of plants and flowers and fruits (where) wild vines...spring to every branch and rock" (John Fletcher Hurst). Effusion! The Victorians didn't fear it.

On the way to Kandy — 1980: Sweltering heat, bus fumes, roaring lorries, motorcycles, kami-kaze drivers trying to pass on the two-lane grade choked with two-way traffic; and the air conditioner has broken down. There's a shriek of brakes. All traffic is flagged to a stop by the police. A cavalcade of Visiting Dignitaries speeds past toward the hills. We make a fast move into last place and in two hours, eyes glued to the road, and oblivious of scenery, we top the grade into Kandy Town.

Kandy Town — 1897: "...coolness and quiet in the midst of scenes as beautiful as the hand of God ever created. 'The fairest view that these eyes of mine ever rested on', said General Booth, speaking of Kandy...How profuse is the bloom from the tops of these trees,...how friendly these hills, how homelike and tranquil these villas embowered in foliage!...the musical drums of the little Buddhist temple amid the trees, by the...tree-shaded lake...a place for perfect dreamy quietness" (John Henry Barrows).

Kandy Town — 1980: Same as above, but read "a *big* Buddhist temple." And he doesn't mention the famous Peradeniya Gardens.

Soon after the British conquered Kandy Sir Joseph Banks, Director of the Royal Botanic Gardens at Kew, had an idea for a tropical experimental garden on the island. The ideal spot was found in 1821 on the Mahaveli Ganga River near Kandy — a loop in the river, at one time the retreat of the Kandy Kings, enclosing more than a hundred acres in a picturesque island. This became the Peradeniya Garden. Begun as a commercial venture to test and acclimatize plants for use in Sri Lanka and other colonies, the garden became, as well, a place of remarkable beauty. Some of the commercial successes were coffee, tea, rubber, cinchona (the quinine tree), vanilla, camphor, cloves, cocoa, and hundreds of medicinal plants. "...considered the finest in the world and no wonder...the tropical luxury, the unthinkable variety of form and freak, the splendour and magnificence of it all..." wrote Clara Kathleen Rogers, a spell-bound visitor in 1903.

The precise word for Kandy is 'spell-binding'. It's in the comfortable scale of the tree-covered hills and the proportions of the lake and the smallness of the town — an intimate and 'eternal' setting that focuses on itself. Our place on Castle Hill, on the steep southern mountain barrier of the valley, faced due north, and was high enough to overlook the town and to see silhouetted against the northern sky, at the precise northward point of the triangular valley, perfectly formed twin mountain peaks, far enough away — some 18 crowmiles — to be veiled by the distance. The peaks, Etipola and Rilagala, top 4,000 feet, and from Kandy Town, at 1,500 feet, they tower as misty gates between the real world out there, and the enchanted valley.

The highlands — the Kandy Fortress of Sri Lanka's embattled history — enjoyed a state of nature well into the 11th century: few people, no 'development' and no 'civilized' centres. Four primitive deities guarded the island — Upuluvan, Saman, Vibhisana and Skanda, some of them of pre-Hindu origins and a goddess, Pattini, guardian of chastity. This quintet had things to themselves except for lonely ascetics and the wild Vedda people hunting the abundant leopards, bear, foxes, elephants, birds and monkeys keeping the hills alive with sound and action. Even now, in the myth-making mood of the high country, every rock looks alive, and trees harbour as much magic as ever Greek trees did. Down on the coasts the lowlanders half believed mountain legends they themselves had invented, and credulous westerners agreed that the island might not be quite of this earth. Marignolli, a noble Tuscan Minorite missionary known as John of Florence, reminiscing about his accidental visit to Sri Lanka in 1342 wrote the famous sentence: "And from Sellan to Paradise, according to what the natives say after the tradition of their fathers, is a distance of 40 Italian miles; so that, 'tis said, the sound of the waters falling from the fountain of Paradise is heard there." His name for Sri Lanka is one of many, that run together and said as a chant, rolls like an incantation: Simoudi-Salike-Sielediva-Sihalam-Serediva-Sielendib-Serendib-Zeilan-Silan-Tamraparni-Taprobane; all but the last two were derived from the Sanskrit name for the lion — Sinhala. Centuries later the Portuguese heard the soft-spoken Sinhalese say 'Sri Lanka' and understood it as 'Ceylon'. As for Tamraparni and Taprobane: Robert Knox reports from his 20 years of captivity in the hills that Tombranee is the name of the Malabars for God. What does one make of that? Paradise?

The slow collapse of the Old Kingdoms inspired entire villages on the northern plains to trek south to the hills. They became hillmen making good use of traditions inherited from more than a thousand years: how to erect earth embankments and control water. They turned hillsides into rice fields, built terraces and diverted streams; on unstable ground they planted tree-crops to hold the earth — all techniques known to their ancestors of the hydraulic civilization of the plains. And these newcomers brought Buddhism to the hills. The faith competed successfully with the Hindu and Animist deities worshipped by the earlier hill people. The old gods may have been intimidating, but they were approachable and open to persuasion, an important point to farming people who hoped to sway the cosmic forces of weather and abundance. In time an accommodation developed; in many, perhaps most, temples the old gods are often worshipped as assistants to the Buddha.

Uprooted noble families retreated to the hills and carved out small fiefdoms; they became the Kandy Chieftains. Joined in a confederation, a hill kingdom called Udarata, they chose one of their number to be King (or they concurred with the wishes of an ambitious Chief). Up to the last, the Kandyan Chiefs reserved their right to approve a new King of Kandy and arm him with the Sword of State. The Chieftains built a small stone and brick temple, called Natha Devale, perhaps as early as 1314, designing it in the Dravidian, the South Indian, style, as a reminder of the Old Kingdoms. The site they chose for their temple was on the bank of a low promontory of the east hill of Kandy Valley near a spring-fed pond, Bogambara Wewa. They followed ancient instructions on the placing of temples: "the Gods sport where water is." The Kings of Kandy were formally approved by the Chiefs in the Natha Devale.

As capital cities in Sri Lanka go, Kandy is a late arrival. Pushed by the Tamils from one undefendable lowland position to another, kings ruled for 30 years from the hill town, Gampola, a dozen miles south west of Kandy. Before 1400 they had moved to the west coast and built a capital at Kotte near Colombo. By 1590 a number of insubstantial claimants vied for the role of King of the Sinhalese. The Portuguese had their candidate; others, cousins and half-brothers, feuded for the honour, and the only kingdom not controlled by the Portuguese was Udarata, the Kandy Kingdom. But of that dynasty only a Princess Royal remained. When the strongest non-royal leader of Udarata was killed in the feuds, his son took up the fight and settled the matter by ambushing the Princess Royal, marrying her and declaring himself ruler of all the Sinhalese: Vimala Dharma Suriya, King of Kandy. He was a skilful schemer and also the possessor of good luck: all the other claimants to the throne died. Vimala Dharma Suriya settled his capital at Kandy Village, then called Senka Degala. It was an astute choice: the valley is protected by narrow passes and by the Mahaveli, the largest river in Sri Lanka.

In Kandy, Vimala Dharma Suriya found himself with a ready-made council: the hereditary feudal Chiefs. Vimala Dharma Suriya conceded a number of privileges to placate them: rubber-stamp approval of future kings, and consultation on State policy. The Chiefs were in no position to argue for Vimala carried with him the true talisman of Sinhalese Kingship, the Sacred Tooth, said to be the Buddha's. How did he get it? That is one of the mysteries. He built a new and larger shrine for the Relics and he built his palace close to the shrine — it was an unwise king who let the Relic out of his sight. Vimala's Temple of the Tooth, the first version of the one now in Kandy, has been rebuilt and restored many times. And in 1930 the Burmese gave as a gift to the temple complex a three storey administration building, providing the final touch to this world show-place of Theravada Buddhism.

Just north of the Temple is a portion of the palace of the last King of Kandy, who transformed the small spring-fed pond called Kiri Muhuda (milky ???) into the half-mile lake we see now. All of the eight palaces built in the 200 years of the Kandy Kings have vanished but for the palace-fragment now used as the Kandy Museum.

In the Museum are sections of columns from the oldest Kandyan hill temples, each labelled with a name that looked unpronounceable until we learned that each letter is sounded and stressed equally; then a baffling string of letters like *Gadaladeniya* became Ga da la de ni ya, and comparatively simple. I emerged from the museum with a list, and a shift in the dimension of our interest in the ancient methods of roofing dagobas.

CHAPTER IV

HOMAGE TO ANCIENT SPLENDOURS

Architectural Note

Colour photo-coverage of the wood shrines of Sri Lanka's 'hill country' has not until now appeared in one place, so a word needs saying that will put it in context. The buildings are close to folk architecture and close in their structural essentials to rudimentary village house construction, and they therefore comprise part of the ancient building tradition of Monsoon Asia which can be traced back at least 2000 years. Monsoon Asia is predominantly rice-growing, bamboo using, and Buddhist and is an immense area which includes parts of India, Nepal, Burma, Bali, and Japan, as well as Sri Lanka itself.

Being of wood, these small buildings are never more than 300 years old, but they provide a living record of that prehistoric architecture which scholars have not yet thoroughly explored. The wood tradition can be shown to go back to Anuradhapura and Polonnaruwa, the stone and brick cities of the north, the former having been first established about 450 BC, while Polonnaruwa saw the height of its power in the 11th and 12th centuries AD.

In the hill country, with a few exceptions such as the stone building at Gadaladeniya and others at Kandy like the Natha Devale and the temple at Galmaduwa, the carpenter and not the mason took the lead. But there was also mixed construction as we saw at Lankatilaka and in one building at Gadaladeniya — both near Kandy. And there are cases of stone columns which are made to imitate wood, as at the small stone temple at Ridi Vihara.

The purest example of the shrine room type, all of wood construction, though supported on short stone piles, is at Medawela where a small verandah encircles the building and a carved doorway affords access. This shrine also illustrates the "Kandyan tiled roof" with its two-angled slope, the break point supported on posts which become the framework for the wattle-and-daub or the masonry wall of the shrine room below.

Both the drumming hall (digge) at Embekke and the Royal Audience Hall (the Mangul Maduwa) at Kandy represent another wood type — the open pillared hall. Above the carved pillars, the cross beams (in a usually box-like skeleton framework), the pillar brackets, and the rafters are often given ornamental carving. At Embekke at the hipped front end of the beautifully crafted roof 26 rafters are tied by the huge ornamental wood pin.

The ancient central building at the Temple of the Tooth, the Dalada Maligawa, at Kandy is the finest. Like the divales at Badulla and Ratnapura it is two-storied, but at Kandy an ambitious architectural purpose comes to the fore. Unfortunately it is impossible to photograph more than its detail because of the closeness of the later surrounding buildings. The inner shrine containing the Tooth is on the upper floor.

Certain factors appear again and again in these traditional buildings: a sharp tiled roof pitch with widely projecting eaves; a highly decorative treatment of the structure both painted and carved, and, occasionally, the decoration of the enclosure walls; the demarking of interior spaces as naves or aisles by closely spaced columns; and the use of stone piles or plinths.

The text voices our initial puzzlement about the roofing (if any) of the masonry stupas and vaulted ceilings of Anuradhapura. We have no final answers, but offer several alternative ideas. As a focus we took the circular Thuparama temple at Anuradhapura and the four concentric circles of stone pillars that surround it. The Vatadage at Polonnaruwa can be subjected to the same speculation. We advance the possibility that the circles of stone columns did not support a roof, but were used instead for the hanging of painted curtains, or for supporting Buddhist symbols, or lamps.

However these guesses are outweighed by the opinions of researchers who believe that there was in fact a wood roof over not only the concentric areas of the stone columns but also over the stupas themselves. Our text and our photographs present two very small and very much later types of wood roofs over masonry — one at Lankatilaka (near Kandy) and the other near Gadaladeniya.

There are said to be linguistic reasons that support these opinions, and the rock-cut temples at Karli, Ajanta, and Ellora in India give parallel inferences. At the Vatadage roof, tiles and iron nails have been found.

The wood shrines of the Kandy hills seem to be the traditional end-product of wood roof types that composed the skyline silhouette and colour of the ancient stone cities of the north, and they exemplify the oldest wood building traditions of Monsoon Asia.

25. Porch to Cave Temple, Ridi Vihara.

26. Library at Padeniya Vihara

27. Padeniya Vihara, lion procession.

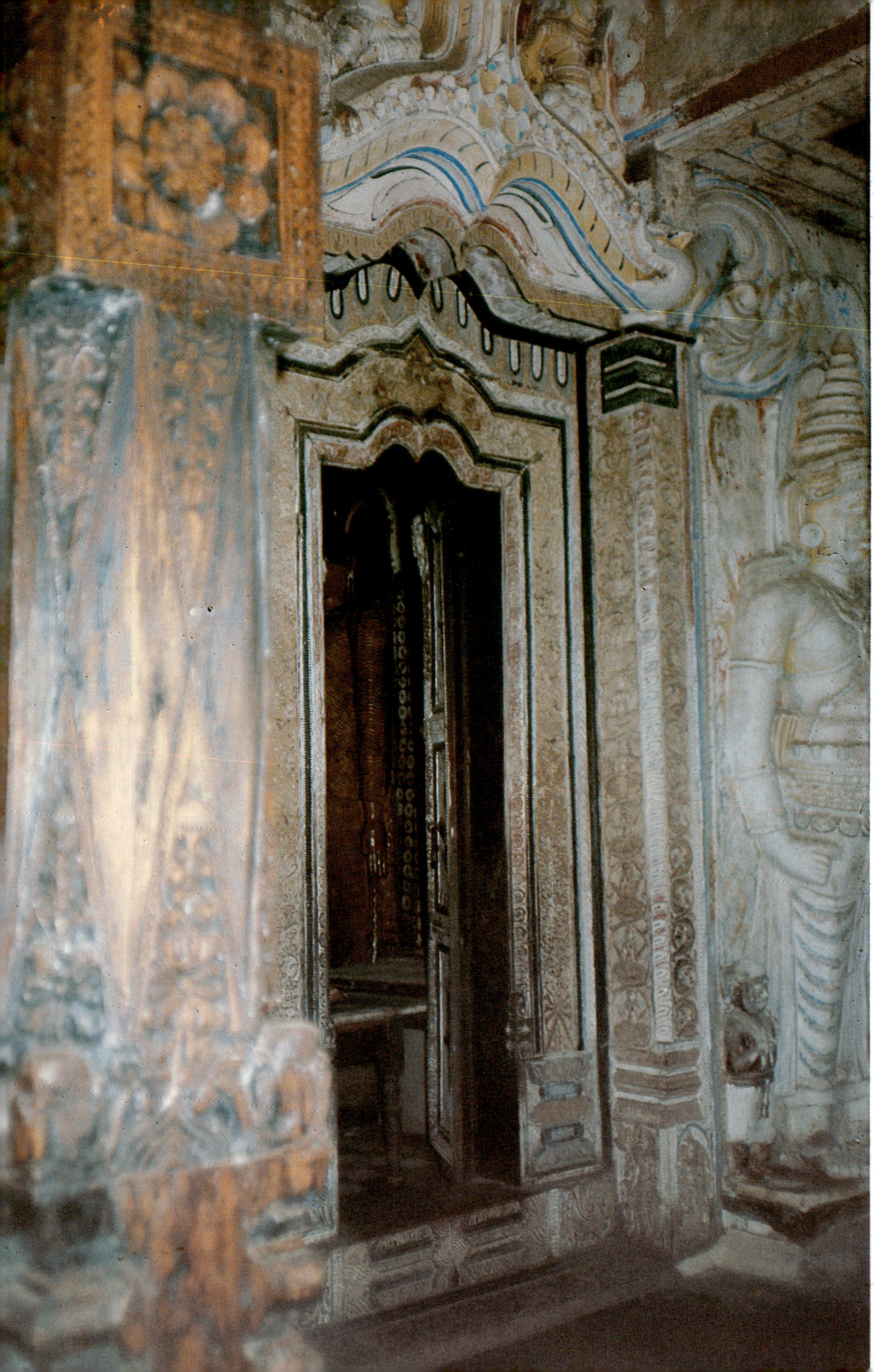

28. Door to inner sanctum, Padeniya.

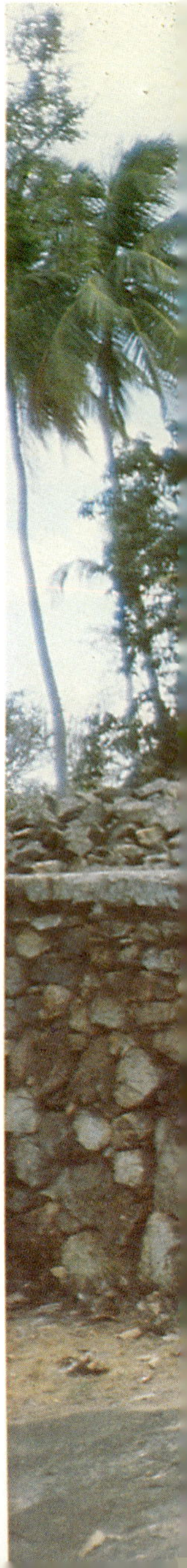

29. Vihara, village style, Kolambagama.

30. Buddha image, Kolambagama.

31. Vihara on "Stilts", Dorbawila.

32. Construction detail, Dorbawila.

34. Pilgrim's rest, Godamunne.

35. Perspective from rear of Shrine. Dodanwela Vihara.

36. Adahana Maluwa Gedige Vihara, Kandy.

38. The Temple of the Tooth, Kandy.

39. Detail, Temple of the Tooth.

40. Detail, Temple of the Tooth.

Of the five temples we saw on our first excursion, the first three, Gadaladeniya, Lankatilaka, and Embekke, looked back to the early days of the Sinhalese retreat to the hills. Each of them is built on an idea brought from the Old Kingdoms: the first using stone, the second, brick. Embekke, built of wood, is an ancient architectural type of construction in the Kandyan tradition, the full flowering of which is in the town of Kandy itself.

Gadaladeniya

The rice terrace valleys are green with young rice and walled by coconut palms rising like green plumes up the sides of the rounded companionable mountains — all in bright winter sunshine. In a few miles the valleys give way to spice gardens. Nearing a village we apply the brakes: the road is striped with wide, spice-coloured bands — the villagers' winter harvest of cardamom, pepper, clove and nutmeg spread to dry. We drive on slowly; each fragrance filters up to us. The villagers and the school children walking in their white uniforms under the roadside trees smile.

One drives uphill through a tapestry of trees, sky, and birds that are camouflaged by their own brilliant greens and blues, and sees an abrupt brown roof-line over the filigree of leaves: the temple, Gadaladeniya, on the top of a small hill of bedrock. We walk up the slope; the small temple appears to be a jut of stone just now punched out of the bedrock by the fist of the rock god, and still daubed with his weatherings and lichen, the lines sharp and clear as broken stone, seven hundred years have not defused its vibrations. The stone walls are finely cut, and not by provincial amateurs (Pl. 1).

It isn't a simple copy of a South Indian temple. They produced a strong architectural individuality by balancing the proportions, and by subduing Indian exuberance. Another surprise in the design: the designer decided on horizontal lines, lines more natural to a building of the plains than to the woods of a hilly landscape where tallness and verticality might have been expected. He attempted to link his stone temple to the forest by carving the stone columns as if they were made of wood...We look behind the temple and see a tall dagoba that is in fact roofed with wood (Pl. 3). Could it be the echo of an ancient idea? On this small dome the square roof settles well enough, but enlarged for the huge dagobas of Anuradhapura...?

A monk unlocked the door of the image-room for us and daylight poured on to a gilded image at least 8 feet tall of the Buddha sitting in a silvery alcove. The sculptor made a stern figure deep in meditation. We left him to his golden light in the darkness (Pl. 2).

Gadaladeniya was built, some say, in 1344, a year close to the great days of medieval Sri Lanka and about the time Ibn Batuta saw the island "raised from the sea like a column of smoke". In the West, the English were raising the spire on Salisbury Cathedral.

Gadaladeniya was built by Rev. Seelavamsa Dharmakirti, the Sangharaja during the reign of Bhuwanekabahu IV (1341-1351 AD). On the rock outcrop on which the temple stands is an inscription of this dignitary regarding its construction. Parakramabahu VI effected repairs. It was constructed by the architect Sri Ganeshvaracharya in the style prevalent then in South India. The structure is made of stone except at the sikhara where the top is built of brick. Rising over the sanctum it begins in an octagonal shape but has been given the features of a dagoba. The vestibule and the porch of the structure have flat roofs. A Buddhist image house is in the sanctum of the main shrine and a devale has been incorporated in this vestibule in a northward extension. On the stereobate at the entrance are figures of musicians and dancers. At the front of the steps at the entrance to the main shrine are a moonstone and two balustrades.

The celebrated scholarly monks such as Dharmakirti II and Vimalakirti I who resided there and contributed much towards the literary development of the country attached their fame to Gadaladeniya.

The main shrine has all the features of an image-house with mandapa and a garbhagriha. The devale and the digge are to its right and project from the mandapa, and the deity worshipped there is identified today as Visnu. The construction of devales within Buddhist temples could have originated in the medieval period.

The image of the Buddha in the garbhagriha according to the inscription was executed on the Vajrasana or adamantine seat under a sacred Bo-tree, here symbolised by a floral design. The Makara torana is decorated on both faces with a host of gods such as Sakra, Brahma, Suyama, Santusita, Natha and Maitri, and two attendants. The upper two storeys are non-functional and form the stone base for the sikhara which is in the shape of a stupa. This type of sikhara is found in the Natha devale as well as at Gedige Viharaya at Adahana Maluwa.

Lankatilaka

One approach to Lankatilaka is up narrow steps built against the 200 foot face of the cliff. We passed that without a pause and kept on round the cliff, driving to the top, and the easy approach — a level path from the village to the temple on a rock rim of space (Pl. 4). Double pitched Kandyan wood roofs hung like dark wings over tall white masonry walls, and the whole bright fantasy hovered above the panorama of the tropical valley. Coming near we saw carved elephants peer from the walls, and forest spirits, serpent gods and twin leviathans on guard at the entrance.

A boy lolled against the steps watching us. "Locked", he said, "monks at lunch." Then he volunteered to go down the cliff for the key. The boy and a young monk toiled up; the monk spoke fluent English — he'd recently come back from London and Paris. He unlocked the sanctum door and sunlight flooded a 10 foot image of the Buddha as a young man, his body gilded, his robes painted cinnabar, jewels around his wrists and fresh white flowers in his hand (Pl. 5). The image has immense charm, young, determined, happy and ever so slightly impatient. On the wall framing him a whole mythology of people, demons and air-creatures coil in smoke and clouds. Above all this vivacity and brightness hangs the dark void of a high brick vault, another echo from the old Lankatilaka on the plains at Polonnaruwa which also has an even more famous brick vault mixed with wood construction and a puzzle to archaeologists.

We walk to the cliff edge and look back at the temple. In imagination we funnel the winds of the past 700 years in one blast and sweep the wood roofs off the temple and we have the Polonnaruwa Lankatilaka — but 'inlittle'...and those sockets in the brick vault, that cause so much speculation at Polonnaruwa, are for the beams of the wood roofs. Had the old stupas on the plains been shafted with sockets to hold wood roof beams? and the holes later filled in?

On the rock outcrop on which this shrine is built is an inscription of Buvaneka Bahu IV (1341-1351 AD) and a Tamil inscription of Wickramabahu IV (1357-1374 AD). The inscriptions inform us that the Vihara was built by the Minister (General) Sanalankadhikera and that the work was executed by the architect Stapati Rayar. Apart from the stereobate the rest of the structure is built of brick. The inner structure here is a Buddhist image house. This has been enclosed on all sides by another structure and the space so obtained has been used to house gods, Upuluvan, Saman, Vibhisana, Skanda and Ganesha and their consorts. It is recorded that the Vihara had originally three storeys. On either side of each entrance on the outer wall are elephant figures of stones in frontal aspect. There are sixteen of these figures in all. In the image house are paintings of the Kandyan period.

Culavamsa says that Parakrama Bahu of Kotte had stucco work carried out at Gadaladeniya and Lankatilaka in the 15th century.

Lankatilaka Viharaya is built of brick and granite on an uneven stone surface. According to the Lankatilaka copper-plate inscription, the original building was 32 cubits or 80 feet high. The building is cruciform. The sanctuary which is a square is enclosed by an outer casing wall leaving circumambulatory space along three sides. On the exterior of each of three sides is a niche in which is placed an image of one of the popular deities of the period. At either side of the entrance are devales. Thus Lankatilaka is a Buduge (image house of the Buddha) as well as a devale (image house of god).

Commenting on its architecture Paranavitana was of the opinion that the temple is "essentially a continuation and development of the Sinhalese architecture of the Polonnaruwa period with some Dravidian and Indo-Chinese features." Taking into consideration all the aspects of the building, when it was entire, he was convinced that it would have been "somewhat similar to that of certain temples in Pagan, in middle Burma, particularly the one called Nagayon dating from the eleventh century." A flight of steps behind the garbha gives access to the second floor which is not used today. The two upper storeys have collapsed and in the restorations the building has been provided with a wooden roof. But in the original building the terrace of the "third floor was surmounted by a stupa in the centre with four smaller stupas on the four corners. The dome of the central stupa was not solid, but contained a circular chamber. The stupas at the corners must have been merely ornamental. At the corners of the first and second storeys now preserved, there were also small stupas, for the corners are rounded."

Embekke

"Anno 1657, the Ann frigate, of London...set sail out of the Downs in the service of the Honourable the English East India Company...to trade from port to port in India...on the 19th November, 1659, happened such a mighty storm, that in it several ships were cast away, and we were forced to cut our main-mast by the board, which so disabled the ship, that she could not proceed in her voyage. Whereupon (she) was ordered...(to) go to Cotiar Bay (in the island of Ceylon) and there to trade, while she lay to set her mast." Twenty years later Robert Knox escaped from 'village-arrest' in the Kandyan hills having been taken prisoner with seventeen other Englishmen for entering the island without permission from the King of Kandy, Rajasinha II. The Dutch had ousted the Portuguese in the six month siege of Colombo two years before; now the King was trying to oust the Dutch and trusted no Europeans. Our road ran through hills where Knox spent the last years of his "sad captivity"...of which he writes: "We were brought up into a town on the top of a mountain called Laggendenny...one of the most dismal places that I have seen upon that land. It stands alone upon the top of a most sad and dismal mountain...In this town we remained three years (then) I chanced to hear of a small piece of land (and) I went on cheerfully with the purchase...the place also liked me wonderously well...cornfields... coconut trees...fruit trees...The price of this land was...five dollars, and a great sum of money...The terms of purchase being concluded, a writing was made upon a leaf after that country manner...I then took possession of the land...some 10 miles southward of Kandy in the town of Elledat..." From 1668 Knox lived eleven years in 'Elledat' before walking away to begin the months of his thrilling escape, the tale that inspired Defoe to write *Robinson Crusoe*.

The road marker bore two names as we got near Embekke — Embekke and Elledatta! We did not know that Knox had lived 11 years across the road from the temple; he doesn't mention it. The deity at Embekke is the War God, Kataragama. 296 years after Knox began his 22 years captivity among the Sinhalese another westerner was 'captured' — by choice. William Hull writes about an American dancer's visit to the island in 1956: "Martha Graham's longest memory of Ceylon will be a drive through the Kandyan countryside, a walk along a narrow path through a grove of cinnamon, clove, coffee and cocoa, giving way to banks of ferns and flowers, down rock steps, through a paddy field and up to the neat village of Embekke and to the Vihara." We went that way, too.

The temple standing alone in a meadow is a mere porch of three open sides a digge for ceremonial drums attached at back to a small building, the temple itself. That, at a glance, is the sum of Embekke and seemed not nearly enough to justify its fame. We went through a low wall to the meadow by way of a roofed entrance portico, an ambalama — a rest house — a little outbuilding with carved stone columns. The path on the right heads to a rock outcrop, called Daulagala, past workshops where today craftsmen carve copies of wood sculpture for the Colombo gift shops. In the left corner of the meadow are well made granaries with wide eaves, raised a foot above ground on heavy timbers (Pl. 9). Finally the path runs to the stone steps of the temple. We walk under the eaves and enter a space much like a forest glade. A double row of columns on either side of it casts tree-trunk shadows on the stone floor. Overhead a skilfully crafted system of beams and rafters reach out, tightly interlaced like tree limbs (Pl. 7). On the beams, columns and brackets are hundreds of relief carvings — flowers, leaves, and miniature scenes of wrestlers, goddesses, mythological bird-beasts, soldiers, farmers — reminding one of the impish figures on the capitals of Gothic columns (Pl. 8). There are over 200, they say, of these tiny tableaux and no two alike.

We studied the miniatures, so tropically exuberant, delighted by the ingenuity of the unknown carvers and the carpenters who perfected their skills and worked out the grace and lightness of this small building those hundreds of years ago. They were the heirs, certainly, of the builders of the old cities: the skilled wood craftsmanship at Embekke was generations in the making. We looked at the fourth wall the wall of the temple sanctum. Two powerful lions moulded in deep relief, painted a stinging yellow, stood on either side of the closed door. On the white wall the two yellow lions sent shock waves through the forest, a fine handling of symbols (Pl. 6).

Europe and Asia spent centuries developing systems of memory-aids — although they used no word as blunt as that. The idea was not only to stimulate the faculty of recollection but to span the gap between the 'mortal' and the 'immortal' by jarring the mind. In the East both sight and hearing were manipulated to call up a desired mood, and also to hurtle devotees either into super-consciousness, or thrust them back to the instincts of infancy. For this purpose one text recommends "images rare or exceptional, shocking, beautiful, grotesque or comic" — and the repetition of hypnotic sounds by instruments or voices — drums, horns, conch shells and chanting — and by movement: dancing.

The two bright beasts at Embekke stand for the lion-father of the Sinhalese: a legend is told that the islanders descend from the union of a goddess and a lion, perhaps Pattini, Goddess of Chastity, and the brave first Sinhala Lion-King, Vijaya? The lions at Embekke are implacable guardians of the old War God; only privileged guests may enter the mysteries beyond the door. Rumour has it that where the walls of the devale rise above the roofline to make a high-ceilinged space, the upper walls slope in and heads of lesser gods look down to an immense painted image holding the centre of the floor.

Some historians believe Embekke was built at about the same time as Gadaladeniya and Lankatilaka — the 14th century. The stonework of the plinth is the work of master stone-masons, and the columns and roof of master carpenters. An argument might be made that these craftsmen came to the hills in the entourage of the kings who established themselves at Gampola a few miles away, and that these master craftsmen were put to work on the three temples. On the plains only buildings of stone and brick have remained to show something of those times. Embekke may be a glimpse of those ancient cities themselves, where, as Fa-Hsien reports, "the dwellings of the merchants are very grand; and the side streets and main thoroughfares are level and well-kept." Could he have added "and lined by houses of carved wood columns and handsome wood and tile roofs?"

Embekke may be the oldest wood building close to its original condition in Sri Lanka; the type of hard wood used for it is impervious to the borer beatle that destroyed other buildings. An official guide came to discuss the protective measures being taken to fight the pest. As we were leaving, he offered to show us a sculpture of a peacock in a wing off the side of the temple. When he opened the door, a python at least twelve feet long and a fore-arm thick uncoiled from the pedestal of the sculpture. We seized our camera, but were unprepared for fast action; the python rapidly disappeared through a hole in the wall, cut to his precise diameter. He completed his vanishing act as our camera clicked on the flick of the tip of his tail.

The story of this devale is told in a poetical work named Embekke Varnanawa in which is explained the role played by King Vikramabahu III, his queen Henakanda Biso Bandara, and a drummer named Rangama in establishing a three storeyed deistic shrine. The date given there is 1371 AD. Today we do not see a three storeyed building here. It is possible that some time later during the Kandyan period it was reconstructed.

According to Embekke Varnanawa the reason for constructing this shrine was a miracle concerned with Rangama drummer and supposed to have been the act of Kataragama deiyo. King Vikramabahu III, apprised of the incident, caused this shrine to be put up in the deity's honour. Henakanda Biso Bandara, the queen, is also associated with this legend. It seems her flower garden was near by. The god, seeing her beauty, released her from her human bonds and made her his consort.

The local tradition holds that the devale was built in the 14th century but it is difficult to believe that the structure is older than the 17th century. The pillars in the digge of the devale and other architectural members are exquisitely carved. Of all the wooden structures of the Kandyan period this can be taken to be the most attractive. We can form an idea of the roofs of the Anuradhapura period by a study of the roof of this building. The upper storey of the sanctum is a false storey without an upper floor. The four walls of this section are supported by four wooden beams. There is a book of folk poems composed in the 17th century on the origin of the devale and its carvings.

Among the ancient objects that are treasured in the devale are the door-ways of the Sandun Kudama which is supposed to have been brought down from the palace of Vikramabahu with the pinnacle seen now on top of the sanctum and the two tusks seen in front of it. The palanquin presented to Rajasinha II by the Portuguese and Tamboruwa drum and ornaments presented to the devale by Ehelapola Maha Adikaram are all treasured here. An Esala Perahera is held here annually drawing large crowds from the neighbouring villages. On the grounds of the devale there is also an old Vee-atuwa or a paddy store resting on stone-pillars and reminiscent of the ancient Temple Viharas.

The Archaeological Department undertook repairs in 1948 and some of the pillars were replaced by the help of local craftsmen, who claim their lineal succession from the original masters, the chief being Delmada Mulachari. The village to the rear is still busy with these craftsmen.

Alutnuwara

An ancient temple on the lowlands beneath the Kadugannawa hills is called by this name. A newer Alutnuwara is in a circle of hills west of Kandy. There we walked up a lane between bedrock banks that had been walled and planted. Along the sides of the lane in grass-roofed shelters copies of sacred objects and paper ornaments — gifts for the temple and mementos — were neatly displayed, simply offered as a convenience, with no sales effort by the vendors. A picturesque pavilion perches on the bank at the top of the lane, and one walks down into the temple courtyard (Pl. 10). But here a clamour of flower peddlers and hawkers of tinsel wreaths swarmed and jostled around us in a frenzy of thrust-fist selling. We escaped up steps and found ourselves at the door of the sanctum, a heavy double-door shut tight. But just then a monk opened the door and smiled at us. We had to respond, and stepping into a dark void, heard the doors close solidly behind us. The sanctum was packed with people listening to its sacred texts intoned by a deep vibrant voice that throbbed and echoed round the walls. Without windows and with little light, the heavy sweet smell of flowers and incense condensed in the air until it seemed too thick to breathe and, backing toward the door, we fumbled with the handles and slid out. A few steps took us to a side exit and the flank of a hill and up a trail that looked out over the on-going festival called Alutnuwara.

Returning past the salesmen we strolled on the lawn. Families sat under the trees, a few young farmers stood beside heaps of fruit to sell to holidayers. We saw a small dagoba and wondered if a snip from one of those hairs of the Buddha, enshrined at the other Alutnuwara, was deep inside it. A scholar has resolved questions about the enormous number of dagobas each "supposed to enshrine a particle, in most cases a minute one, of the corporeal remains of the Buddha". He says, "The sceptic may wonder how bodily relics of a Teacher who lived in this world some two thousand five hundred years ago can be obtained now, but for the faithful it is a matter of no great difficulty to procure what is believed to be a genuine relic of the Master, whenever a new stupa (dagoba) is founded."

A tiny woman approached the shrine beside the dagoba. Leaning her parcel against the pedestal she reverently placed one yellow flower on the shrine, then dropped to her knees (Pl. 11).

Not far from the dagoba an old temple is being "restored" by a group of local painters and craftsmen. The walls and ceilings and bas-relief figures had been freshly stuccoed but not yet decorated with colours and the room wore a veil of austerely beautiful whiteness. A smoothly plastered image of the Buddha appeared to sit on a white cloud which soon would have its subtleties obliterated under layers of primary colours. From the space of whites we turned a corner to watch a painter laying on the wall the first strokes of paint of a sleeping Buddha. Alutnuwara gave us a look at on-going temple life.

Dodantale Vihara

A large stone slab spans a stream to a small travellers' shelter. The trail winds on along the slope above a green, rice valley; large boulders edge the hill face, and shrubs and trees on the valley side frame views of the fields where farmers bend at work. The dry smell of cut rice straw put a dash of bitters in to the sweetness of the green perfumes. On the slope fifty feet ahead movement caught our eyes and we stood still. A four foot land lizard slithered possessively about a field of rice-straw, saw us and stopped, then, slowly, with the hauteur of a dinosaur, walked up the hill and vanished among the trees.

Over the centuries farmers have shaped the valley to flood their fields, striking thin dikes at the proper gradients across the valley and fitting them with stone sluice valves. The dikes are footpaths as well, compacted by centuries of footwork. Halfway across we stopped and looked down-valley admiring the wide cascade of the land fall. Looking up-valley the surge of terraces swept toward us — we were standing midstream in a static flood that was channelled between hills originally carved by the untamed waters.

On the far side we were among coconut palms and banana groves...there's a rustling in the palms — is it monkeys? Then a small brown leg slides down. Little boys hidden among the fronds are cutting the nuts and letting them fall...

From the slopes behind the cultivated groves, the jungle sends in tantalizers...butterflies; flashes of jewelled plumage and loud snippets of birdsong. Neat minute houses appear at intervals along the trail, each set off by a proper garden and flowers. For all the forest in full bloom about them, the Sinhalese love their gardens. In small houses all over Sri Lanka fresh flowers sit in jars or little vases, and every day at dawn flowers are taken to the neighbourhood temple.

The stone slabs that lead from the trail up through the tangle are obviously steps to the big white building just visible at the top. It looks like a house, but on the roof is a brass finial — the deserted place is the temple, Dodantale Vihara. There are no fresh flowers here. On a high verandah the interior walls of a former sanctum are painted to show a sinister court reception...life size figures outlined by broad dark strokes and shades of dull red made lurid by dabs and patches of white, and some of the faces almost obliterated with black paint. These are of the last king of Kandy, his queens and courtiers, standing below a row of seated saints; and they, too, are painted in a hurried, impressionistic way (Pl. 12). The brush strokes reflect his people's lack of reverence for the infamous king, Sri Vickrama Raja Sinha, who built the Kandy Lake and the big pink temple; he of the gruesome pleasures.

The first steps down to the path banish the tyrant's evil presence. Joy and innocence overwhelm worldly shadows on the trail through that blissful landscape. Farther on, beside the trail, lay a high flat rock, and, wanting to linger in paradise, we climbed to the top and stretched out in the shade of overhanging palms — a time-stopping moment when all was right with our world. The breeze filters the sunshine on the warm rock; only a few miles away was Kandy — but for a while, we were part of a time that could be a thousand years ago.

The notes of a flute lifted lightly in the sunlight a stream of pure tones pouring from an invisible player closeby. We dared not stir fearing he might stop, but listened for fifteen minutes to a lilting, delicate, space creating melody, touched with as sweet a tristesse as birdsong. We climbed down and went toward the music. The flutist stood on a flat rock with his family nearby, wife, father and children. A farmer musician, proud of and loving his music (Pl. 13). The handcrafted flute was of fine wood fitted with small embossed metal pieces, a beautiful thing. We asked him to play again and had a second concert. We learned that he went to the temple to play for ceremonies, but to us he'd brought the temple with him to the field.

The farm people had left the fields and gathered along the roads to gossip and laugh, and spicy smoke from cooking fires drifted on the evening air as we drove back through the hills. In Kandy the shops were closed and the setting sun splashed the big temple with a coral-red light. Somewhere we had read: "It is the search for treasure no less than the treasure itself which makes life worthwhile." We had had something of each on our first excursion.

CHAPTER V

IN THE COOL MOUNTAIN AIR

"In the afternoon I came over a very wild and mountainous country, through which the government are now laying out, and making a graded and macadamized road...at immense labour...it is cut into the sides of the mountains...very steep...most of which appears to be a sort of gravelly quartz, with gneiss, and now and then piles of blue granite...(which) must be cut down many feet or entirely removed by blasting." Miron Winslow made the trip from Kandy Town to Nuwera Eliya (pronounced Newraylia) in 1820 by stagecoach, palanquin and on foot. A hundred and sixty years later the road is an engineering masterpiece of elbow turns and switch backs, rising 3,000 feet in ten miles. Improving on Winslow's three and a half days we covered the distance in five hours, as awe struck by the scenery as he when he described the second day of his trip: "The...road this morning was through what is called the "dark forest"...much like thick primitive forests of heavy beech and maple. (Then) it runs along the side of a steep mountain...bare of timber...the grandest mountain scene which I ever witnessed. On the left...a high barren cliff...almost perpendicular; at some distance another...in the form of a vast round tower with dark and dilapidated walls, and...high mountains of the most fantastic forms...immense piles of light and dark...rock so disposed as to (appear like) a town in ruins. (Below...runs) a long narrow beautiful valley — rich fields...terraced beds...now and then a native house...a few trees or a garden...a small river winds...receiving contributions from all the surrounding mountains...there are no less than five waterfalls in view from one point...all the mixture of wildness and loveliness...made this panoramic view exceedingly impressive." The wildness and loveliness is still there — rock walls and falling water, and eagles soaring far below us in the shadows of the canyons. Winslow travelled on, topped the cliff-road, and came to "a mountain...thickly wooded, the trees large and tall..." But Anuradha and I went into cut-over eroded mountains, the trees cleared almost a century ago, first for coffee plantations, then when a blight hit them, for tea. Now the slope he saw is a rocky, scrub-covered stretch laid out in tea plantations.

Good things came to Sri Lanka in the 19th century when a plantation economy was superimposed on to the old peasant economy: roads, trains, processing plants, and the back-up developments of the technical training of staff and labour to support large scale agriculture. As benefits, these have to be weighed against the loss of forests — the stripping of the high central slopes. Even on the lowlands the primal vegetation has almost disappeared; reserves and private patches are all that remain of vast, always-green forests. For the moment the mid-high hills of the Kandy district enjoy their woodlands almost intact and the soil is deep. But the shallow soils of the high ridges are under-laid by impermeable rock, and each year the torrential rains send run-off floods down hill with no forests to stop them. Plantation clearing has sharply increased erosion and flooding, an old problem originally created by generations of farmers clearing forest by fire. Notwithstanding their skills on the mid-mountain slopes and on the plains, farmers knew nothing about soil-analysis and the unrestorable nature of the top plateaux. The big new dam rising at Victoria Falls near Kandy should prevent floods in the lowlands.

We swung to the top of Ramboda Pass and looked out over the Nuwara Eliya plain. We had left the rice fields and palm trees far behind. Up here in the cool mountain air, the grass covered valley circled below us. A small river banked by masses of rhododendrons trailed south past groves of conifers somewhat like Scotch pines. Driving down through the savanna-like grassland we were depressed by the thought that this valley and the high plains further south had once been covered by dense primeval forests, every tree laboriously burned off in a few centuries in the hope of producing croplands. But the cropland, leached by a single generation of monsoons, was abandoned and permanent damage was done. Now the grass is too anaemic even for grazing without the expense of heavy fertilizing. What with the early peasant farmers and the 19th century planters, Sri Lanka was becoming another Crete — which, too, was once a wooded, spring-splashed island. Thanks to hindsight, reforestation is on this island's priority list.

Near Nuwara Eliya the English gardens begin, and the English houses, small and half-timbered, settled among roses, hollyhocks, sweet peas; many of them are a bit run down since the change from those well tended days when this was the Queen of hill stations. A last refuge from change is the old Hill Club and its famous golf course, and the portraits of illustrious members of the past, and the faultless service.

But we must revert again to ancient times. The stories of Sita and her abduction by the ten-headed demon king of Lanka, Ravana, are still alive in this area for it was in Nuwara Eliya that Sita was kept hidden by Ravana after taking her away from Rama. The battle between the two took place on this soil.

It was just about here that we turned off to go to Pusulpitiya Temple.

Pusulpitiya

North east of Ekneligoda the road lies on a narrow meadow between steep jungle-covered valley walls. In a few miles we turned into a side track for another brush with the legend of the famous Sacred Tooth Relic of the Buddha now enshrined at Kandy.

Months before, we had walked among the 3rd century pillars of the Sacred Tooth's first shrine at Anuradhapura, and at Polonnaruwa, the spectacular 10th century ruins of the second temple to this mysterious relic that is at the heart of Buddhist Sri Lanka. In its journeys the Relic once had been hidden for 17 years in a place called Pusulpitiya.

The side track pointed straight up through the jungle; Pusulpitiya was above us. Decades ago, a road had been laid down and there were remnants of surfacing, but the jungle resented even that, and whipped the car with branches as we struggled up hill. The going was too steep, the engine boiled, coughed and stopped. We took to the steep trail, surfacing a quarter hour later in a temple courtyard — merely two small temples and a house. Anuradha, a Sinhalese scholar, renewed acquaintances with the resident monk, and two boys were despatched to fill the car with water, while we looked at the temples. The larger temple had been 'restored' to dull plainness, but the smaller had a whimsical air, decorated with painted guardian swordsmen and a dragon, a sun with eyes, a pensive moon and two rows of skulls; the little building beamed with a 'jungly' forest charm. The larger, the principal temple, was dim inside, the one window letting in a pale wash of light. A glass case in the centre of the room housed a small dark image of the Buddha surrounded by silvery objects glowing mysteriously in the gloom; a hanging divided the room. Drawing it aside the monk invited us into the unlit space behind. The floor was cluttered; boards, chunks of stone and sections of plaster had been pulled down in the search for the niche where the Sacred Tooth in its casket had been walled up — the niche was about the size of a car battery. Before leaving the temple we looked from the window. In the valley far below a massive rock rose some thousand feet from the woods and meadows of the valley floor where the prince who had hidden the Relic at Pusulpitiya to ensure victory in his fight for the Kandy throne vanquished the king's forces.

A burst of laughter in the courtyard — the boys who had gone to fill the car had forgotten to take a bucket. We all went down and filled it from the brook.

This temple belongs to Uda Bulatgama and is situated about three miles from Morape on the bank of the Kotmale Oya. The area is full of folk legends as it was the place where Dutugemunu, the hero King of the Sinhalese, spent his boyhood.

The origin of the Pusulpitiya Village and the Viharaya is related in a Sinhalese folk legend which has pusul gediya or ash pumpkin as its central theme. The village as well as the Viharaya is named after this ash pumpkin.

According to another legend, one of four valuable Buddha statues brought by an Arahant named Maliyadeva from India is now deposited in this Viharaya. The temple is historically linked with the Sacred Tooth Relic given hidden security here during the times of political unrest in the country. During the Magha rule at Polonnaruwa in the 12th century it is reported that the Tooth Relic was hidden here. King Vijayabahu III (1232-1236 AD) of Dambadeniya came to Kotmale and removed it to his capital. Again, when the British were about to enter the Kandyan Kingdom, the Tooth Relic was hidden in this temple. The British found it there and brought it back to Kandy immediately after the capture of the Kandyan Kingdom in 1815.

The Bogoda Bridge

The narrow unsurfaced side road edged off the plateau into a steep valley under hill-hugging trees. Waterfalls and brooks flowed across the track. At last the way became so narrow that a slip could spell disaster; we abandoned the car and often passed little houses clinging to the side of the track on a patch of farm — a minute rice field, a few vegetables and a cow. Birds sang, but the ceiling of leaves hid the singers; at a clearing we could look below into the valley.

41. Balustrade, Temple of the Tooth, Kandy.

42. Entrance interior, Royal Palace, Kandy.

43. Roof of Royal Audience Hall, Kandy.

45. Classic Kandyan roof structure. Audience Hall, Kandy.

46. Elephant in Kandy Town.

47. The scools at the Malwatte Monastery, Kandy.

48. Our view from Castle Hill, Kandy.

The trail ended at a flight of downward steps, irregular stones laid at a steep angle. We edged down, and, looking to the right, saw a long covered bridge spanning the gorge as delicately as a dragonfly poised on leaves.

This was Bogoda, a clearing above a rocky stream at the foot of an immense rock wall. A recess at the base of the rock wall had been deepened then enclosed to make a temple, the Bogoda Vihara. Beside the temple was the monk's house. He came to meet us — an old, dignified man suffering from goitre who courteously conducted us into the cave; in the dark an image of the Buddha lay asleep against the base of the overhanging rock. There was a charmed mood at Bogoda — the isolation, the stream, the trees, and under the stupendous rock a sleeping image cared for by a suffering monk.

We walked across the bridge, a plain roofed structure supported by two piles struck into the bed of the gorge. The beams were low, the railings a bit flimsy, but the 'feel' of the bridge was sturdy with the strength of fragility, a structure made to lift above the flood and not obstruct it (Pls. 14, 15). From the middle of the bridge we looked down at the large boulders studding the stream bed — water-smoothed boulders shaped like grey-brown fabulous animals. The ghost of a trail went up the far side and vanished among the rocks and shrubs.

Beginning the climb to the car we looked back. Why had this carefully crafted structure been roofed? There was no engineering need for it. Perhaps it was because they knew how to build a roof, the sheer pleasure of using the architectural skills of a tradition going back to prehistory. The little bridge stood among the trees of the gorge, ephemeral and human and confident.

Kataragama Devale of Badulla

The tops of far off mountains were just visible on the horizon of the sweeping highland landscape of well tended farmland. 'Close to Badulla the road widened to take the traffic generated by this district town, and the road was lined with shops. Then more shops crowded around and we'd arrived. Breeching the line of shops, a wide covered gateway led to a wide green lane with a white temple at the top. The high porch of the temple, an airy place of bright white walls and carved dark wood columns, stood above a mist softened view of valley and mountains (Pl. 16).

From the porch we rounded a corner and came to a full stop: a procession was in progress along the wall — on the long wall of the shrine a marvellously painted parade of elephants, monks, sacred objects in levitation, and dignitaries proceeded at a stately pace (Pls. 17, 18, 19). Vividly real, but light-years away from realism, the painting moved in strong lines of banners and staves penetrating the earth colours of the people, animals, objects and deities. The painter understood the delineation of movement, and the forms and slashing lines have moved grandly round the three exterior walls of the shrine for centuries.

The murals of Badulla show how architecture and the architectural arts blend in the Kandyan tradition. The temple's image room, the shrine is the natural focus of the temple. The room must be windowless and closed. The exterior walls of the shrine become spaces for sacred paintings; the paintings are protected in this rainy climate by the wide overhanging eaves supported on columns and brackets. Badulla produces even more interesting effects: the sharp dark strokes in the murals intermix with the strong dark accent of the building's columns; the rhythmic shapes of the eaves driptiles repeat the mural's sacred objects; added to these interplays, the paintings of people and animals and deities are symbols of kinship...the whole has the impact of a counterpoint of living things in space and time.

The mountain roads had taken us from one scenic delight to another. But mile after mile from Badulla westward the avenue of enormous rain-trees had been butchered away. Some of the stumps still smoked. The rain-trees of Sri Lanka are old and beautiful and important to the island. Yet the trees are felled with the spurious excuse of road improvement. There are local bureaucratic and "entrepreneurial" patterns that seldom vary. A local firewood contractor begins a campaign to exploit this source of wood and cuts a few limbs. Then he lodges formal complaints: the trees are "too near the road" and "a hazard for the lorries". He next asks the District Road Office to mark them for visibility. A team of men blazes each tree from root to shoulder height, paints the cut surfaces white and lops off over-road limbs. Many trees deteriorate under this treatment. The contractor then easily persuades local officials that the avenue is "a danger", the road needs widening, and of course, department crews should be kept busy. These facts are presented to Colombo. After consideration a government order is issued and the trees felled. Business people, especially the travel firms, are alarmed, and have made efforts to stop the disfiguring of Sri Lanka's finest roadways. But the make-work programmes of a few years ago, and ever present bureaucratic pressures, seem to override their voices.

Fifteen miles on, approaching Haputale we escaped this depressing reminder of modern times and climbed to the highest escarpment of the island. To the south beyond the green of the lower forests the vales shaded into blue. Out in the blue haze the Indian Ocean stretched to Antarctica and the invisible Equator streaked round the earth changing the spin of water and wind. On lower hills tea plantations, luxuriantly green, basked in the late afternoon. The whole superb topography lay before us lit by the slanting rays of the sun. At dawn next day we strolled between dewy banks of roses hearing sweet birds sing. The first-light revealed the land falling sharply away near the point called World's End where the drop off is nearly 5,000 feet. Looking east the sky and sea merged in a veil and we saw the winter sun rise out of the mist, floating up calmly from the invisible rim of the distant ocean.

The road to Ratnapura angles west down the mountain. Stone retaining walls face the hillside and a low stone guard-wall edges the drop to the coastlands and the rolling panorama of lower crests streaked by the dawn sun.

Ratnapura

Ratna is the word for jewel, and *Pura* for city — the name of a town, and now used as well for the district anciently called Sabaragamuwa, a province celebrated for precious stones. It is a rugged ridge-and-valley country lying at about 1,000 feet, sharing topography and climate with both the mountains and the coast.

The first mention of the gems of 'Taprobane' came to the West from Alexander the Great's famous admiral Onesicritus. Several centuries later Sinhalese ambassadors to the Roman court of Claudius boasted about their homeland's rubies and sapphires, coral and pearls. China traded silks for jewels and spice; and Fa-Hsien describes Vedda tribesmen in Anuradhapura laying out gems for sale or trade, each marked with its price. He reported an image of the Buddha of green jade twenty cubits high, and rich works of gold, silver and precious stones; at an elaborate ceremony he saw the king dedicate to a new shrine two prize oxen with their horns decorated with gold and gems. Later on, the Moor, Ibn Batuta, an admirer of women (it is said he had 18 wives worldwide), commented: "All the women in the island of Ceylon possess necklaces of precious stones of diverse colours; they wear them, also at their hands and feet, in the form of bracelets and anklets. The concubines of the sultan make a network of gems and wear it on their heads. I have seen on the forehead of the white elephant several of these precious stones, each of which was larger than a hen's egg. I likewise saw in the possession of (the Sultan) a ruby dish as large as the palm of the hand...(and a) statue... of gold the size of a man. In place of eyes it had two large rubies...that...shone by night like two lamps." A few years before the Moor's eyes beheld these marvels, the Italian Friar Odoric heard about a lake "the bottom (of which) is full of precious stones."

Reports of jewels grew ever more extravagant as traders and travellers and finally tourists discovered the abundance of gems, and as quick-witted Sinhalese dealers learned to augment the natural output. 20th century finds are in famous collections: a 135 carat star ruby; the Bismarck sapphire; the 425 carat Logan sapphire, largest of its kind; and within the last few years a huge Alexandrite, one of the world's most valuable stones. Many if not most of these glamorous objects were lifted from the alluvial deposits around Ratnapura; on our way there we passed one of these gem mines.

It was hard to imagine that glittering centuries were adorned from dismal pits like this one. Men were bent double in watery mud up to their knees, groping about, literally coated all over with the pale mud. Gem bearing gravel is collected in baskets and sorted later, but stones of gem quality are rare, the material is usually low-grade, industrial corundum, the impure version of alumina that when pure is sapphire or ruby. The grubby scene we looked at was a commercial mine, a pit, braced and spanned with timbers, dug into a grain field. Other more attractive spots can be privately leased, neater pits with the gambler's excitement of mining fields on the even-odds that the spade may turn up nothing or a sapphire worth a small fortune.

The ancient god, Saman, the brother of the Indian god Rama, may have been worshipped on the island long before Hindu Brahmins came with Vijaya and the Aryan nobles, or the Buddha's missionaries brought his message. Some historians guess that men lived in Sri Lanka a half million years ago. Nearer readings of bits of bone and stone tools put it between 10,000 and 1,000 BC. Saman would have resided here in those times on his 7,300 foot pyramid-shaped mountain, Samantakutha, the island's most famous and most sacred peak. Before recorded history a shrine to the glory of Saman stood on a hill near Ratnapura, less than ten air-line miles from his mountain, a shrine that guarded the pass and overlooked the valley. In the 16th century the strategic location, and their drive against paganism, inspired the Portuguese to pull it down and build a fort on the ruins.

The Dutch, in their turn, ignored local religious customs and had no need for a fort. The Sinhalese demolished the fort, constructed a stone wall around the now sizeable mound of rubble, carried up earth and stone to make a high platform, and built on it a new shrine to their old god, Saman: the present temple of Maha Saman Devale, near Ratnapura.

Thus far the wood temples we've seen were of interest for good things taken separately: the carpentering of the roof, or the carvings or wall paintings, or a marvellously picturesque setting. In none of them had the idea of 'sequential' architecture in space been developed by the intentional organisation of the parts of a single building, or of the units of groups of buildings, in such a way that the parts were related dramatically to each other — high roofs near lower roofs, towers with colonnades and walls at different levels of the site. Now, at the Maha Saman Devale, these complex spatial architectural adventures had been achieved (Pl. 20).

First, the exterior roadside walls hid the courtyard completely, so the big court came as a surprise, not only for its size but for the island of buildings looming behind it, buildings raised on the platform of walls with roofs sharp-angled against the sky. Then in the courtyard, as if tossed there at random, were a sacred Bo-tree, a sculpted stone of strange shape and no known meaning, possibly a relic of Portuguese rule, and a tall, peak-roofed, free standing ceremonial pavilion. Two tiers of roofed viewing terraces fronted the temple island, and a long flight of steps ending at a dark wood door in the white wall of the temple.

We climbed the steps, enjoying backward glances at the changing pattern of roofs and tree and gate, opened the door. Then we entered the roofed loggia and looked out at another surprise: a two-storeyed temple surrounded by a quiet sunny courtyard. Two small temples stood in the court, and enclosing everything was a fine roofed wall fitted with large windows so passers-by on the road outside could see the temple. The court was carpeted with small amber-coloured stones, and the shrubs growing along the white wall stood out clear and dark in the warm serenity.

We were admiring the little courtyard sacred to Pattini, Goddess of Chastity — a handsome miniature building in the best of the Kandyan tradition with figures on the walls under the porch roof painted so vividly they appeared to sway and shimmer in the shadows (Pl. 21), when a worshipper came up the front steps into the loggia, and a monk came to conduct him to the Image Room. We went along.

The long axial arrangement of the buildings immediately became apparent — the whole plan made itself felt, and the 'energy' of the parts as they followed each other on the temple island. We remembered the narrow and high facade of the Shrine Hall and now we saw its sweeping length. Here was the farthest reach of the temple, and climax of the visual drives we'd hoped for, consciously or not, when we first came to the roadside gateway.

The monk opened a small door, entered with the three of us and closed the door. Inside after a mysterious moment of darkness our eyes adjusted a dark curtain hung just in front of us. The monk turned to us and implied that a non-Buddhist should step back against the wall. The monk and the worshipper spoke quickly together and suddenly the man was on his knees before the curtain and for a split second the monk flicked it aside and the man looked up beyond the curtain at...what?

The Walawwa of Ekneligoda

Settled among the wooded hills not far from Ratnapura is a random arrangement of well-kept streets, gardens and tropical houses — the town of Ekneligoda. The largest house in town is the Walawwa, the Manor House. The family who own it were at one time the feudal chieftains of that part of the valley. The house is believed to be 300 years old, going back to such days, but seems today to be a contemporary piece of artistry: broad, red tile roofs and white columns, wide cool verandahs on two levels divided by the rows of columns that outlined large spaces. There are inner courts and big rooms and the finishing and furnishings are handsome: ebony and cane, polished dark stone floors, teakwood ceilings; on the white walls hang bold paintings by modern Sinhalese artists; on shelves and in cabinets are ancient objects from the family's collection; inner rooms are lit by ingenious lightwells open to the roof — a 'contemporary' idea designed with the house in the 17th century! On the porch of an inner court is a magnificent table, the top a single solid slab of wood tapered like the tree itself from a four foot width narrowing for seventeen feet to a three foot width of continuous grain, the slight ripple polished to a stain lustre (Pl. 22). We had tea there, put together with great style by the master of the house himself. The house and the people in it seemed effortless and unselfconscious.

This elegant, graceful atmosphere is to be found not only in manor houses. On a later trip to the north a typical village house caught our eye and we stopped to ask if the owners would allow us to see it. They were surprised but very warm and courteous, although we soon discovered we had come at a difficult time. Like the big house at Ekneligoda, this small house had an airy immaculate tropical charm. The building showed some of the wood tradition now often used by modern Sinhalese architects; there were recesses in the walls for lamps, the wall along the verandah had been stepped to give an irregular silhouette and the roof had a steep pitch with open rafters and brackets. We asked to see the kitchen and our host took us through the central room of the house. Then we discovered that their mother, a woman of great age, was nearing her last days. She lay in the main room, close to the come and go of the family. Returning through the central room from the kitchen — which proved to be simple and practical with an open fire and pounded earth floor, new aluminium and enamel utensils in rows clean and orderly — we were struck again by the serenity of the fresh white walls and windows shaded by flowering vines. The woman lay on a neat grass mat on the earth floor — houses in rural Sri Lanka have no furniture as we know it, everything was spotless; — her white hair brushed smooth, her white sari smooth and carefully arranged, her eyes were closed, her posture tranquil. Just a few days more...but she rested peacefully in the heart of her family.

A New Bridge and the Peak

The valley narrowed as we approached Kandy through the Ginigathena Gap. Our driver swung into a side road, stopped and pointed to a small bridge over the river, and looked back smiling in expectation of some remark from us. We were puzzled and said nothing. The driver lost his smile. "You see this bridge before?" We shook our heads. He shook his head in disbelief. "This bridge a famous film bridge, the Bridge Over River Kwai." We were sorry to have fallen in his esteem, but his next surprise for us came off better.

We were going through the rich foothills of the valley of the Mahaveli Ganga. At one point the trees opened out and the driver pulled to the side and pointed toward the mountains on the east..."Adam's Peak!" He looked back anxiously to see if that famous name registered with us. We laughed and got out to look at it. Adam's Peak, the old Samantakuta where the indigenous god, Saman, has lived forever, is such a touted island show piece that we expected to be disappointed, and stared sceptically at the horizon. But we couldn't mistake the pyramid among the lower rounded peaks. Early seafarers agreed with the islanders that it could only be magical. Those tough old sailors considered the peak one of the wonders of the world: "for although situated twenty leagues from the sea, on a clear day sailors could see it some distance out to sea..." a pyramid floating on clouds.

The first Moorish sailors were so struck they at once realised it to be the point where Adam brought Eve when they were expelled from Eden; they believed that Adam stepped first on to the peak, being the nearest earthly place to the Garden of Paradise, and, with one foot on the peak and the other in heaven a final surge of heavenly power pressed his earthly foot deep into the stone; they climbed and found a "footprint" to prove it.

According to the principal Sinhalese chronicle, the Mahavamsa, the Buddha, at the invitation of God Saman, stepped onto the peak at his first visit to Ceylon, eight months after his Enlightenment on "...that full moon night...of the month of Vesakha (May)...at Bodh Gaya" about the year 528 BC. During his call on the deity the Buddha granted to him some hair relics which the god enshrined at the dagoba quickly founded for the purpose at Mahiyangama. Buddhists recognise the footprint on the peak as the Buddha's; and furthermore the pyramidal form is a prime symbol to them of the tree of universal life. In its turn, the Hindus suggest the print is that of their supreme Siva.

The footprint, very much larger than life, whosoever it may be, is actually there and pilgrims of most of the world's faiths have climbed to see it. Ibn Batuta, who wrote so much about Serendib, describes his ascent of Adam's Peak in 1344: "The people of old have cut in the rock steps of a kind, by the help of which you ascend; fixed into them are iron stanchions to which are suspended chains, so that one can hold on to them...the chains of profession of faith, so named because a person who has reached the top and looks back at the foot of the mountain will be seized with hallucinations and fear of falling." There are chains still in place and people who climb to the top these days use words very much like that.

From the top of the peak a strange phenomena sometimes occurs at dawn. The evening before pilgrims climb up carrying tapers — a ribbon of lights moves up the mountain. They sit all night, meditate and listen to the chant of monks. The sun's first rays strike the peak. The shadow of a perfect pyramid appears in the west sky — valley mists have risen to make a blue screen. The other awe-inspiring event, realists say, is the getting down again from the top of the mountain. The descent seems almost perpendicular, and some people refuse to budge while those with a head for heights must crawl over them until they're coaxed to bump down from step to step; it is often two hours up and four down.

CHAPTER VI

TEMPLES ON SACRED STONES

The Mahaveli Ganga

The Mahaveli Ganga, Great Sandy River, moves through the dramas of its sculptured valleys from its source on the 6,000 foot Horton Plain to its rendezvous with the Bay of Bengal near Trincomalee. Skirting the plateaux at the west side and gathering reinforcements, broad and deep it elbows round Kandy — in the old days a useful "moat" for the Kandy Fortress. Now, hundreds motor, walk or bike daily over the three bridges near Kandy town. The main road north from Kandy crosses by a long bridge and follows the river for a half mile, a stretch known as the Elephant Bath. Numbers of pachyderms lie on their sides in the shallows, some enjoying a good scrub, others dozing comfortably with a selection of brushes laid out on their round bodies while the scrub boys gossip on the bank. Farther along parties of women wash clothes, banging them against flat dhobi-stones. The women will be in high spirits chatting and pounding, blithe and pretty — the bright saris, bright water splashing, with wet coloured fabrics in the sun. The road divides at the bridge: the north branch ends 140 miles on, at the Old Kingdoms to the north. A branch west goes to the town of Kurunegala and then the coast. The river takes its own erratic way south, then east, and is joined by important tributaries for the final run flowing easily on the plains northeast to the sea.

In 1955 an American diplomat, Philip Kingsland Crowe, a keen sportsman, on a three day journey in two 30 foot canoes, tackled the last 60 miles of the Mahaveli Ganga: "By 11.30 we left the last cultivation and started through virgin jungle, lush tangles of great trees, cable-like creepers and matted grass...the banks had been crushed down as if by a giant bulldozer and in the mud were the huge platter-like impressions of elephant feet...The ever-new fascination of sailing through untouched wilderness made up for lack of lunch...beer tastes good anytime...on a jungle river it takes on the quality of nectar...crashes of branches indicated that an elephant or a sambhar deer had started away. There are crocodiles...most of which are

man-eaters. We spotted two huge elephants (and were) cautioned not
to make a noise, (in) several cases they had charged straight at canoes,
capsized them and then tried to locate the terror-stricken (people) by
smelling them out...We drifted down silently on the pair...I drew back
the hammer on the .405 — just in case...The country is full of bears and
leopards, (and in the river) giant snakeheads weighing over 20 pounds
(these are) air breathing fish which...surface every five minutes...(On)
the last stretch of the river...sunken logs, whirlpools and
rapids...brought frenzied action from the crew...We had some close
calls but got through without...a brush with the crocodiles!"

One could probably repeat that trip today.

Medawala Vihara

West of the Kandy bridge a steep road winds up through rich hilly
farmland. International advisors who report on agriculture to the
government consider the farmers of the Kurunegala District equal to
the Japanese in producing high yields from their small holdings. A
mere three-tenths of an acre — with a stream on it — will supply
coconuts, rice, fish, vegetables and fruit, supporting a family in
comparative comfort. Almost 60 per cent of the farms are owned by the
farmers who have inherited their lands down the generations; the
well-known pride of ownership is a great spur to their energies. The
people looked prosperous — in terms of a 'low cash' economy they are
entered no doubt on the poverty statistics. But the rich land yields
year-round crops, fruits drop into their laps; they have vegetables and
flowers. Where people have food, health and happiness, it shows on
their faces, and how do statisticians tabulate that?

When the earth as we know it was being jostled into position from
300 to 150 million years ago (according to Hoyle, Sir Fred, FRS) Sri
Lanka is shown on speculative maps as the final but separate vertebrae
of the spine of India; and when India, riding north through the seas as
a continental plate, collided with the Eurasian land block, the tail
buckled into the remarkable folded rock cliffs and canyon valleys north
of Kandy where we were driving.

Among these north-sloped hills and vales was a temple, the
Medawala Vihara, at the top of a tall rock cliff fronted by a flight of brick
steps built up straight to the discouraging height of the ridge. A few
deep breaths and we tackled them. Struggling up we came to a
diversion, a ledge that centuries ago had a cave hollowed into the rock

face to make a temple, of interest only because the mystique of caves is deeply-rooted in both Buddhism and Hinduism. Finally at the top we were rewarded by a small handsome wood temple raised on a stone plinth (Pl. 23). Every detail of this remote small building was in the best of the tradition. This temple is the classic Kandy type. No monk appeared; we tried the door; the temple was firmly locked.

Here at Medawala was an ancient vihara where a three storeyed image house was built by a king who reigned at Dedigama. When this building fell into disrepair the present temple on pillars was built there by King Kirti Sri Rajasinghe. The temple is reared on short stone pillars supporting a plank floor on which is the image house which has a three foot ambulatory all round it. The image house has wattle and daub walls and a carved wooden door frame. On either side of the door are two janitor figures. Inside is an image of the Buddha seated under a torana. On the walls are depicted figures of gods, the Vessantara and the Uraga Jataka stories. The moonstone, the stone steps and the Gajasinha balustrades placed at a door giving access to the rear image house at the premises seem to belong to Dedigama times, the end of the 14th century or the early 15th century.

Although this ancient temple is traditionally believed to have been founded by King Valagambahu (103 BC) all that is now within the irregularly shaped enclosure — a dagoba, vihara, Bo-tree and platform — belong to the Kandyan period. According to the Medawala Sannasa it was built by Kirti Sri Rajasinha in the year 1755 AD. The vihara stands on short stone pillars and is therefore called a Tempita Vihara.

Ridi Vihara

The road, shown on the map as a cart track far from any main road, rises steeply through the honeyed landscape, passes a village, makes a sharp climb and without warning stubs against a rise. From here a path angles up the face of a wooded promontory, rounds a shoulder of the cliff...nearby is a temple that could have come from ancient Anuradhapura. The temple is stone, but the carvers had laboured to duplicate wood in many details — columns and the way structural parts were handled all said 'wood architecture' — showing the great age of Sri Lanka's tradition of building with wood: the tradition begun and husbanded thousands of years had come to full flower before this stone copy could have been conceived. It was a lonely 'outlandish' copy of the courtly ways, even to the silhouette against the sky, and trees of a gateway that led to nowhere, a piece of landscaping, a 'folly'.

The hills, a thin cover of earth and shrubs gave way to bedrock, and the trail, a wide natural inclined ledge, curved up the steep promontory, the great stone cheek of a rounded eminence above the valley floor. The ledge widened. A long and narrow house, its back to the cliff, brightened the trail by a verandah of carved pillars lacquered yellow and red, the monk's house, and the colours winked like sparks struck from stone (Pl. 24).

The trail widened still more and rounded the hill to a temple settled apparently by magic below a fifty foot heap of boulders, big irregular stones with faded paintings on them. Part of this vihara was a cave dedicated to snakes; we were not expected to go in (Pl. 25). Further on, in another cave, a powerful Buddha image stared down without a hint of compassion for the human race. How had the image — this masterpiece — so alive, 'appeared' to the sculptor? Buddhists cultivate a detached state of mind. The image was said to have great sanctity. Next round the hill was a plain temple with handsome ivory inlays, very old, above the door frame. In the sanctum of the temple: another Buddha image of unusually spiritual force, but this the sculptor had shaped with a deep but unsentimental compassion. The image ignored its phalanx of intertwined dragons, steaming demons and other excited symbols. That shrine was at the end of the trail on the stone hill; the whole hill is a composite temple, Ridi Vihara, built up over 1700 years, from 200 BC to the 16th century.

Here is the Rajatalena Vihara established by Amanda Gamiri Abhaya (19-20 AD) where inscriptions of 2nd century BC up to 8th century AD are found. Today in the premises are remains which range between the 12th to 13th centuries.

Padeniya

In Sri Lanka, so close to the Equator, the days are almost equally divided in light and dark — 6 am sun-up, 6 pm sundown, give or take a few minutes, and at noon the sun is straight above us the year round. We drove down the grade from Ridi Vihara at high noon, the sun directly overhead and our shadows were black spots at our feet. We were travelling with friends, one a monk who owns the templed hill. Each of us had brought a lunch, and we expected to sit in the car, eat and move on. But that was not how it is done: the monk sat alone in the car, water was poured over his hands, and each of us went off in a different direction to sit at our separate places until we thought the monk should have finished — the monk must eat first. After a reasonable time on a rock above a pond, we two ate our cold chicken and looked at the winsome landscape until the slap of sandals on the path set us in motion toward the car. A delightful lunch, somewhat unstructured, but flavoured by the experience of being part of an ancient ritual.

From the soft air of the hills to the plains in the bleakness of the dry season; small farms, and on the ponds — perhaps fragments of the old water system — choked with weeds and stagnant, the strange jacana birds teetered about on the water, the black and white dazzle of their plumage flashed on the bleached, bedraggled farmscape.

Trees fringed the road, dry country trees, then at a distance and clear of the trees lay a long low plinth of bedrock as big as a city block. A number of plain buildings dotted the rock and backdrop of pale trees grew beyond it. This was Padeniya. There was no imposing silhouette, no special feature, only steps and a gateway, a tree and a path — it seemed unpromising. The path divided: one way went toward a rambling house, the monks' house; the other up the slope of the rock.

The slope was easy and levelled off in a dozen strides near a Bo-tree. The roots hugged the rock, and bits of a crumbled stone terrace, who knows how ancient, embedded in the trunk had been pulled up over centuries by the growing tree to four feet above the level of the rock — a rich confusion of roots, stones, fragments of masonry. A new stone terrace ringed the base: the tree seemed to be emerging from the very bedrock. And the new terrace — a new act in the slow moving drama — will be engulfed and raised high, and in a future age offer unreadable messages to that day from ours. Minute silver and purple banners were tied all over the tree, and fresh flowers scattered round it — perfuming the air...gifts from the monks and the local people to the tree and the rock. On a lower slope of the rock deep fissures almost too wide to jump were filled with diamond clear water — as far down as we could look there was no bottom to them.

Midway on the rock a small building stood by itself, an ancient library not in use, and, without the usual careful crafting of wood, it had been put together in a rough and rugged way; plaster crudely stroked on to the heavy masonry, and rough-hewn wood beams shaped by a few strokes of an axe into a token frame over the door (Pl. 26). Inside, the scheme of several levels and open spaces was seen at a glance, and steep pitched ceilings were, except for the cramped scale, familiar California split-level planning. The second floor had been used, after the library closed, for grain storage, and large bins fitted with heavy covers inserted into the floor. We lifted a cover and a mongoose jumped out. No one could imagine how he came there.

At the far end of the rock: a roof with a brass finial — the Padeniya temple. From a distance it was notably unremarkable, but closer we could see a frieze of lions crouched along the top of the white wall deep under the eaves. Moulded almost round and painted with pulsing colours, they swarmed there, roaring, creating a mystical barrier round the four walls that enclosed the sanctum (Pl. 27). The sanctum itself was merely a free-standing hut under the central pitch of the roof. But the hut had been transformed by a stroke of fantasy: an elaborate wood pergola surrounded the shrine door. Columns with carved brackets held up a sloping lattice, and the whole painted with gleaming brown. This framework was topped by a flat ceiling, coffered and modelled with elaborate foliage, and painted sharp white. Below the fanfare of dark and light the sanctum door and side panels were painted with electrifying and radiant purples and mauves (Pl. 28). The space crackled with colour and high style contrasts. The door to the sanctum, however, was locked. The carvings on the wood pillars are comparable to those at Embekke.

Not far from the temple, the edge of the rock overlooks a lotus pond. Trees arch over the water, kingfishers dive, orioles sing, bustling among the leaves, barbets tap out the seconds of the day and parakeets screech to each other. We leaned out and the whole wild aviary flashed up in alarm and swung away in a rush of colour to distant trees. We walked back to the entrance gate, sat on the stone and looked at the Bo-tree again. The roots would be deep, very deep, and the springs welling up near the tree? They are part of the lotus pond at the other end, both welling from a source far down under Padeniya rock.

The three monks of Padeniya were men of erudition who carried themselves like Roman senators. Their large house was spare, the rooms airy and lined with books and portfolios, their furniture — a few fine pieces of old Dutch teakwood and cane...an unworldly retreat, as serene and dignified as the men themselves.

Kolambagama

Several hundred years ago at the beginning of the 'Kandy Period', about 1600, the villagers of Kolambagama believed the natural rock plinth near their village should be crowned by their own village temple. Instead of appealing to the Chief or to Buddhist priests they designed and built it themselves. At great effort large boulders were brought and laid on the rock to form a rectangle, and tree trunks shaped into beams were put across the stones. On them a small hut, the temple, was built. That is the legend of the beginnings of Kolambagama Devale, and the effect of the little building among the palms, archaic and unstudied, makes this account believable (Pl. 29). The exterior has the look of villagers' work; the inside is a different matter. Packed into the cramped space are original ideas: two carved and painted pillars with brackets richly shaped as drooping blossoms, a stylized lion guardian painted in black, like the pillars and brackets; black pottery objects and jars, a type no longer made. But the treasure of Kolambagama is a standing Buddha image; merely of stucco and paint, folk art in every way, but within its limits the image compares favourably with the bronze Buddhas of north India — a unique, universal quality, the Buddha shown abstractly, with the face of a man in action in the world, a man with an active mind (Pl. 30). Too often modern renderings of the Buddha are slightly vacuous in spirit, even sentimental. Kolambagama's Buddha is alive with spiritual force.

Dorabawila

On the jungle cart tracks among the palms another small, very old and unusual temple, Dorabawila, has been raised — this time well above head height — on slender, rough-cut stone piers (Pl. 31). The high flying little building is vibrant and lively in the pattern of its roof line with whimsical brass birds perched on the ridges, and the fringe of leaf-like driptiles, also the well crafted interlocking timber joints of the cantilevered balcony — another earth grown temple as natural to its setting as the people and the trees (Pl. 32).

Ancient paintings and Buddha images are found at this temple on pillars. The wooden carvings and the roof have the special characteristics of the Kandy period.

Niyamgampaya

History and legend indicate that this was once an important place of worship and a centre of Buddhist activities. But the present remains do not help us to reconstruct its past. In the main shrine the plinth mouldings of the old structure have bas-reliefs representing musicians, dancers, drummers, animals, and lotus designs (Pl. 33). The valuable Buddha image was stolen in 1907 and has not been traced.

Trees and Architecture

We have seen that the very ancient buildings of the north which remain to us are of brick and stone, but some of these show evidence of an earlier history in wood. And where primeval forests still flourish and modern ways have not overwhelmed tradition, delicate, elegant wood buildings flicker with the magic of trees. Some of the loveliest and least known of these are in Sri Lanka, direct links to the buildings of prehistory.

The story of mankind is linked to trees, the first secure dwellings, and to forests, a most hospitable habitat. At different times over millions of years the progenitors of humans lived in fernlands, vast forests, broad savannahs and mountains. Those forces helped to shape humanity but a most profound influence was the forest. Even now we retain forms, skills and senses developed on our long journey and instinctively we keep our emotional response to trees.

The evolution of those skills, which occurred even before the development of agriculture, and our feeling for trees can be briefly suggested: branches laced together became a roof upheld by limbs and trunk. (Umbrellas are small portable trees.) Then tree-form shelters were constructed on the ground. The earliest people seem to have chosen to live in a temperate climate on forested land. When, through circumstances, people began to inhabit deserts, saplings were carried to support hide shelters. Wood was treasured and, where scarce, substitutes of bone or stone were used and often altered to resemble wood.

An understanding of structure and of wood construction will have partly come from trees and their root foundations. Forests taught elements of architecture: compression, cantilever, building within the force of gravity, the arching of space and the aesthetics of interior space.

Religions developed the implications of trees: the "Tree of Life" became the emblem of eternal growth. The "Family Tree" gives continuity to the living:

Eche mans a plant; and every tree
Like man, is subject to mortality.

These branches dead & fallen away are gone
From us until the Resurrection.

> Inscription. 1627
> St. Andrews Church
> Chippenham, Wiltshire
> England.

We are reassured intuitively by the vaulted cathedral form or temple form. Our music is often the organised sound of wind in trees, we make musical instruments with wood.

We plant trees by the graves of our dead and so shelter them in the shadows of prehistory.

"And as the Phoenix rises from the ashes so the tree of life grows...from the ashes...The spire of the dagoba represents this tree of life with its higher worlds...Thus the spiritual rebirth of the world starts in the mind of man and the tree of life grows out of his own heart...the tree of life sprouts and develops within him and spreads its branches in ever new infinities; in fact he himself turns into a tree of life and enlightenment." Anagarika Govinda then quotes a 17th century German mystic:

> "Shall the life tree free thee
> From death and strife,
> Thyself must turn divine
> A tree of life."

And Tolkien's modern fantasy has built its magic city in the great "fletted" trees of Loriem, a city of dwellings compounded of dreams from the prehistoric memory abyss and symbols of an overarching eternity.

In the real world, that filtered light, those glints of green and gold, that sense of a time gone that will come again, lively, innocent and always fresh, we see in these tree-form temples.

The wood buildings of Sri Lanka are no older than some 300 years at most. Wood is not permanent in the tropics, but faithful continuities have been preserved by rebuilding as in Japan. More especially the conscious copying in stone of certain wood roof forms and details can be seen in the very oldest of stone structures in the ancient cities of Ceylon — just as it can be seen in the Parthenon in Athens.

These Sri Lankan buildings are a high point of expression in Monsoon Asia of interrelationships of a form and function in this regional setting.

It will take a reverent and thoroughly Buddhist scholarship to trace the processes of stylistic change in the buildings of the hill country and to interpret the aesthetics of Kandyan wood architecture in historical terms. Then these small bright works of Sri Lanka can be placed in proper perspective.

The form, both spiritual and physical, that reflects the aesthetics and ceremonies of buildings must always be inseparable from their religious purpose, with the housing of the image of the Buddha. This is the single key to the building programme — but similar building materials and similar climates the world around tend to produce related results.

Medieval wood roofs of Europe are, many of them, double pitched like the Kandyan. And the wide, pointed Romanesque arches of southern France resemble the pointed brick vaults of the ancient Pagan in Burma. There was no need — nor possibility — of borrowing; the law of gravity, the timber, the brick, the rain or snow often lead to similar answers.

Nevertheless a style of building which soundly incorporates these elements may firmly establish itself in a *regional* setting. This has happened in the Kandyan hills with the "Kandyan roof". The steep central pitch needs little bracing. It is composed of box-like frames. The sharp break in roof pitch that allows for wider verandahs and a shelter for worshippers invariably occurs at a line of columns and these in turn become the slender elements of a spatial screen — each of the many columns is a small unit. Today, often with insufficient reason, the Kandyan roof becomes a mannerism. But understood as good-structure, traditional ornament will emerge from the structure itself, not applied, but integral. And this is what has happened over the centuries in the Kandyan hills.

CHAPTER VII

THE INNER CIRCLE

Godamunne Ambalama

Pilgrims' rests may be as old as south Asian civilization. Asoka, the greatest emperor of India — some historians say of the world — in about 230 BC issued orders carved on stone or iron columns, for the planting of avenues of trees and for building shelters, for the comfort of pilgrims. Asoka was following a tradition of his forbears founded by kings from the Code of Manu of prehistoric times. These meritorious acts of the ancient kings withered away on time's wind, even as Asoka's great palace on the Ganges River, described by contemporaries as built with wood columns sheathed in beaten gold and harbouring aviaries of brilliantly coloured singing birds.

Wayfarer's rests on Sri Lanka, many of them several hundreds of years old, have been kept close to their youth by the continuous replacements of decaying parts and are among the oldest wood structures on the island. Prominent families of a locality will donate and maintain a shelter, or they are put up by the villagers as a place to rest and meet. A close look at a map of the Sri Lankan hills tells without words the intimate part these ambalamas play in village life: on one section of land 3 miles by 2 miles, there are in one instance 7 ambalamas and 9 shrines.

One at least of the small shelters is a minor work of art; the Godamunne ambalama has charm and poise. The roof is square and like a tiled umbrella covers a stone platform about the size of a king-size bed (Pl. 34). The construction is simple: merely four huge foundation timbers joined to make a rectangle that has been raised to seat height from the stone plinth on four big boulders; four columns at the corners support heavy plain beams grained like watered silk, that support the roof. Its carved wooden pillars are damaged to some extent by having been chipped away with knives. It is said that the wooden pillars of the Hangurangketa palace destroyed by fire by the Dutch in the 17th century were used for the construction of this wayside resting house. The British soldiers who camped in the neighbourhood after the anti-British rebellion of 1818 have used this as an abattoir. Placed on a rise overlooking a valley of rice fields near Kandy it is a tranquil, timeless little haven from a tropical downpour.

Rajasinha II, sixth king of the Udarata (the old name for the Kandyan Kingdom), the tyrant who captured the Englishman, Robert Knox, in 1657, was an astute ruler who managed to fend off both the Portuguese and the Dutch. Rajasinha was one of the few kings of Kandy whose palace was not burned to the ground by either the Dutch or the Portuguese. Both his father and grandfather lost so many fair palaces in Kandy that they at last put up sham palaces that would keep the rain off but could be quickly evacuated in a crisis. Rajasinha, however, with justifiable confidence, built not only a substantial Kandy palace, but an additional palace pleasance down river at Hanguranketa. The king relied on a spy network that reported every move in the hills and intercepted every letter. Nothing got past them. His strategies followed closely the Six Positions of Diplomacy as satirically proclaimed in the Panchtantra story by the *King* of the Owls in dealing with the enemy, the Crows, namely: Peace, War, Change of Base, Entrenchment, Alliances and Duplicity. Rajasinha went through all of them, and when Robert Knox fell into his hands he was engaged in Duplicity. He appeared to encourage European trade, but European ambassadors who managed to slip past the Dutch monopoly guards and came to Kandy to talk business found themselves detained indefinitely although in princely style, provided with maid or men companions as they preferred, but allowed no contact with their governments or families. Knox describes the king: he "loved animals, was a good swimmer and horseman and did not persecute Christians, although he was not free from some of the vices of the Roman Emperors. His mother was a Catholic, his father an ex-Buddhist monk and his wife, from whom he lived apart, a Hindu." In fact no wives were permitted in Kandy, even those of the dignitaries who lived at court. Knox says the king was "...a firm, able ruler (who) kept his crown for 52 years...a shrewd tactician." As he grew older he became disillusioned and whimsical. Having aided the Dutch to dislodge the Portuguese (see Positions of Diplomacy — Five) he complained he had "given pepper and got ginger." "The King", says Knox, "taketh great delight...to see his captive ambassadors brought before him in fine apparel, their swords at their sides, with great state and honour..." He kept one miserable ambassador at a village not far from the riverside palace at Hanguranketa — and that brings us back to the ambalama at Godamunne. The villagers there say that during one foray against Kandy, the Dutch set fire to the Hanguranketa palace, and townspeople rescued from the flames the four carved columns now in the little shelter at Godamunne.

Dalukgolla

There's an exhilaration in penetrating the Kandyan countryside searching for temples, and those on a spiral course round Kandy have features that are original and important.

On the road southwest of Kandy, beyond the row of shops and hutments of the suburbs, at an elbow turn in a village within sight of the big river, is an old shrine, Dalukgolla. Up a flight of harshly restored steps and in front of a dagoba built for the ashes of the notable priest, Rev. Welivita Saranankara, there is a high verandah furnished with a vivid confusion of shapes pulsing with colour. The eaves, driptiles, columns, wall sculptures of heavenly guardsmen, and a strange cage-like frame of black metal used for the journeys of the image, are painted and highlighted with shades of earth pigments: umber, raw ochre, black, white and gold. The sun strikes the verandah floor and ricochets into the shadows under the wide roof, lighting the whole collage from below, so that the static pantomime seems to be alive and moving.

Dodanwela

When Rajasinha II was on his way to Balana to give battle to the Portuguese, the cross bar of his palanquin is said to have snapped and he had to alight at Dodanwela. He inquired what the place was and was told that it was Nahimige Kovila. Then the King made a vow that if he succeeded in the expedition he would present his crown and jewels to the Kovila on his return. The King was victorious and the promise was kept. Thus the Kovila became known as Dodanwela Devale (Pl. 35). Dedicated to a local god in the past, it is now dedicated to god Visnu. The avenue of na trees (iron wood trees) close by has adorned the devale precincts for centuries and is protected under Antiquities Ordinance. The crown was deposited in the Kandy museum but later stolen.

Aludeniya

According to tradition this Vihara was built by Mayim Bandara during the reign of Bhuvanekabahu IV. The Vihara itself is not so interesting from the point of view of architecture. But a wooden door-frame called Ranbewa beautifully carved with floral and vegetable designs with friezes of dancers, musicians, images of couples and flying gandharvas which has been placed at the entrance to the Visnu Devale of the temple catches the eye. It is said that this door-frame was brought here from the palace of Bhuvanekabahu. This door-frame can be regarded as the "earliest example of wood carving which has so far come to light in Sri Lanka."

Degaldoruwa

This is a cave temple built by Rajasinha, the younger brother of Kirti Sri Rajasinha, in 1771 AD at the foot of a rock mass about 40 feet high. In the inner part of the Vihara is a large recumbent image of the Buddha. On the rock summit is the old Bo-tree and the Dagoba. The Pitiye Devale which had been built about a hundred years ago is no more. The Degaldoruwa copper plate grant of Rajadhi Rajasinha explaining the work carried out at Degaldoruwa says: It is thus clear that this temple was constructed by Rajadhi Rajasinha before ascending the throne, and that the Sannasa granting lands was issued after he became King. Many of the items described in the Sannasa are to be seen in the temple except the paintings in the Mandapa which has undergone repairs. However, the paintings still to be seen in the rock cut Vihara have been executed by a painter monk named Devaragampola Silvatenne. All this is a treasure-store for the student of art history. Commenting on these paintings Siri Gunasinghe says: "Degaldoruwa murals are considered the outstanding examples of this style of painting. Particularly significant is the well articulated line work which is used very decoratively. Equally effective are the brilliant red backgrounds which set off the lighter figures to great advantage. In this particular scene one could notice a sufficiently eloquent narrative quality both in the crowded grouping and the change in the direction of movement of figures, the turning with gifts and a very unusual use of blue. This was very likely intended to produce this special effect. A strong narrative sense can also be detected in the expressive forward tilt of the bodies of those receiving the gifts. It is not difficult to contrast the impressive look on the face of Vessantara with the eagerness for those waiting to receive the gifts or with the sense of satisfaction on the faces of those who are returning with gifts, especially of the woman. Particularly significant is the ornamental role of the architectural decoration as well as the lotuses filling the empty spaces."

Galmaduwa Vihara

A boy ran down the road and the driver called to him in Sinhalese "Where's Galmaduwa Vihara?" The boy answered proudly in English "Come!" and raced away. We followed and saw him point through the trees to the top of a square, tapered, stone tower. The boy bounded on for half a block, then overcome by curiosity and beaming with good will, ran back just as we photographed the vihara. He grinned wider than ever, waved to us, and kept on about his business.

Galmaduwa juts up alone in a neglected field. A tower such as this originally would have been the imposing focus for a group of religious buildings, a monument intended to be seen as a piece of sculpture. If buildings were once around it they have vanished, and at some time in the past, to provide an enclosed space for temple rituals, the ground floor of the tower was enclosed by a wall, and a roof added from the wall to the tower — an effect, unexpected and bizarre. The tower itself is a hollow shell, and to look up into it, is an upsidedown adventure — tier upon tier of interior corbels are each painted a different colour and design; the look up is like looking down — down into a deep narrowing well.

As its name suggests this is a stone pavilion. Tradition ascribes this place to Kirti Sri Rajasinha who is said to have stopped its completion. The story goes that while it was still unfinished the king heard of the discovery of a cave at Degaldoruwa and so stopped the work on Galmaduwa. This building was never used as a temple though there is a small Vihara to which offerings are made.

The lower storey of Galmaduwa is built of stone and the upper storeys of brick and stone masonry in seven diminishing stages. It is 60 feet square at the base, tapering at the top and hence is called a gedige. Around this is a rectangular stone porch with arches. No doubt it has a strong resemblance to Hindu architecture. The vimana which is described as a gedige features the architecture of Tanjore. J.P. Lewis writes that:

> "Galmaduwa Vihara probably enjoys the unique distinction of being the most Hindu-looking Buddhist temple in existence."

KANDY

We circled Kandy on the country roads, stopping at small temples: Huduhumpola, Kulugammana, Dodanwela. And so we came to the core of the matter: the temples of Kandy town.

Kataragama Devale is in the heart of the bazaar. Inching through the bustling energy of the crowd — avoiding shoe repair men and trinket vendors at pavement level and errand boys on the run, coming to a full stop with eyes shut to give right of way to a fast bicycle, adjusting our ears to horns, shouts, brake squeals, bells, the clatter and shuffle of sandals, the amplified disco-beat of electioneers, the unidentifiable cacophony from the shoulder to shoulder shops each no more than a door and adjacent window — at last we were nodded toward a half-open gate in the commercial facade, and we pushed through. Three steps inside the gate and village calm took over as if the bazaar had been banished by magic. Twenty feet from the big-town furore, the wood temple with its Bo-tree, neat compound, trimmed shrubs and slow pulse showed us the village heart of Kandy — a typical village vihara.

Asgiriya Monastery and Temples

Kandy's business district has grown to fill the triangle of level land below the surrounding hills. Just north of the clanging maze of shops, a wide smooth road goes up the west hill. This fine road is the route of the Great Perahera of the August Moon. The peraheras come rolling down the hill from the Asgiriya Monastery and its neighbouring viharas. The hills are thickly wooded, but the top was cleared centuries ago for the monastery compound, an immaculate square enclosing plain white, yellow-trimmed buildings set off by doors of inlaid woods and bright paint, handsome as jewels. On the hill above the compound are two temples that make up the Asgiriya Vihara and are called New Vihara and Old Vihara, although, naturally, the New Vihara is the older one. From a section of the New Vihara wall plaster has been removed to reveal early inscriptions incised in the stone. The same serene colours and the same fine doors are at the temples as at the Monastery, and the same melancholy mood.

In August there's no melancholy...the Great Perahera procession assembles here with some 100 elephants milling about and a near mile of dancers, drummers and dignitaries sorting themselves out. Night falls and the procession begins to spill down the hill — "Imagine... these huge beasts...decorated with rich trappings...Buddhist priests in yellow robes borne along on portable shrines...devil dancers in fantastic costumes...wearing huge hideous masks...noble headmen... (the) long procession lit up by torches innumerable which burn with a bright glare that turns every...figure into...an artist's model" (Henry Steele Olcott, 1881). The colourful, clangorous river pours down to flood the courtyard of the Adahana Maluwa Gedige Vihara, the Vijayasundararana, a cheerfully solemn building of stone and brick, the second oldest in Kandy (Pl. 36), set under palms and flowering trees and topped by a dagoba dome later roofed with wood. We follow the route of the Great Perahera toward the sacred centre: ...Trincomalee Road — the main street — then turning left before the King's pavilion where now the heads of government and their guests sit to watch the splendours of the August Moon festival, then along the side of the lake and into Palace Square in front of the Temple of the Tooth, the Dalada Maligawa.

Natha Devale

A low shoulder of the east hill extends into the valley before the Temple of the Tooth. Long ago a wide cut was made through it, dividing the temple precinct into two high courtyards; the wide cut became a ceremonial centre called Palace Square, both sides of it faced with stone retaining walls and ceremonial stairways, and along the wall on the side in front of the Temple of the Tooth is an ornamental moat while on the west side of the square, in its own high courtyard, is Kandy's oldest shrine, the Natha Devale, built by the old Kandy Chieftains. Steps go up from the Palace Square to Natha Devale, but the historic way is through a stepped gateway on the town side of the temple (Pl. 37). The Gate is strange and imposing, the lower part, of stone, is perhaps as old as the devale, the upper part is new brick masonry stuccoed and painted a warm yellow, and the gate has been more recently topped by a Kandyan roof.

Imagine this spot in the 14th century: trees and wilderness; a path mounting the low knoll; then against the sky and distant hills, standing alone among the valley trees the tower of a small temple cast in the strong mould and character of South India. The Natha Devale is grey and mossy, still proud and strong, ignoring the nondescript newcomers that press it on all sides. The knoll has become a paved court with a few old trees and many small sanctuaries and shrines where monks sit to expound ancient texts and to chant. Crowds wander about or sit under the trees to listen late into the night; then the courtyard is lit by scores of small lights. In the afternoon, in the shadow of a tree you may see an elephant feeding on a tika branch holding it down with his massive foot. His chains rattle and rock the tree when he curls his trunk round a strip of the soft wood and pulls it straight into his mouth. If you pause to look, he'll notice you and swing toward you. We left abruptly.

Hatara Devale, or the four devales in the city, have a long association with the Royal Palace and the Temple of the Tooth Relic and have been held sacred by the Buddhists and the Hindus alike from their very inception. Of these the oldest is Natha which directly faces the Dalada Maligawa. It dates back to the 14th century and was built by Vikramabahu III. The god Natha to whom a deistic shrine was dedicated is taken to be the power deity who influenced the political affairs at the time. He is none other than Avalokitesvara Natha, a Bodhisatva of Mahayana Buddhism, highly respected and venerated even today by the Buddhists of Nepal, Tibet, China and Japan. He was known to the people as the Senkadagala Devindu or the guardian god of Senkadagala and also as the Buddha-to-be. The shrine dedicated to him shows the influence of the Dravidian school of architecture specially that of Vijayanagar, and is built in the architectural style known in Sinhalese as gedige.

Apart from the Devale in these premises is a small dagoba, a bodhi tree, and an image house, the last of these is not of great antiquity. The gedige, a stone structure built in Dravidian style, may be the oldest structure in Kandy. It has a dagoba shaped sikhara. The ceremonies of naming the king and of handing him the royal sword were held in this building during the time of Kandy kings.

The Dalada Maligawa

It is said the sacred tooth was kept secret for 900 years — between 500 BC and 400 AD; carried off by ship in a girl's hair; twice enshrined in huge stone purpose-built monuments; hidden for 7 years between two grindstones; twice stolen by raiders and carried far away; ransomed by royal delegations; burned and restored whole; stirred wars, fratricide, and patricide; lay walled up for 17 years in a forest hideaway; carried in procession (when not in hiding) each year for 1580 years; became the palladium of kingship; legitimised the rule of kings; tilted the destiny of a nation; inspired countless reports of miracles. It lies now on a gold casket in the innermost of a nest of 7 jewelled caskets in the richest shrine of Sri Lanka and enjoys a lively reputation for miraculous power bringing rain for the seasons, protection for the people, and other undocumented feats. This is the Dalada – the Sacred Tooth Relic, believed to be that of the Buddha. Many legends of the Sacred Tooth are far from substantiated but its part played in history is fact.

When the British at last conquered the Kandyan Kingdom in 1817 one of the Chieftains is reported to have said that "in his opinion and in that of the people in general, the taking of the Relic was of infinitely more importance (than their victory in battle), a sign of the destiny of the British people to rule the Kandyans." The Tooth had been spirited away by a few monks in the early days of the British advance. How they captured the Relic was not known.

The Relic has been in Kandy's Temple of the Tooth for almost 400 years and the Temple has changed shape and colour many times. Sometimes it is white but in 1980 it was a pleasant light coral-pink, a blossom pink, and lovely on the green hillside (Pl. 38). To go in, we cross the bridge over the moat and climb wide steps proportioned for the feet of elephants. There is a crowd of guides. Most of them students from Peradeniya University, polite young men, who take charge of us, check our shoes and lead the way. We go into a courtyard toward a small building as brilliant as a jewel box. Every cantilevered bracket is carved and painted with flowers or tendrils and the ceiling is a painted lacework of blossoms, butterflies, birds, lions, shells, dancers and fabulous things, picked out by staccato points of colour, principally shades of red with white, black and gold (Pls. 39, 40, 41).

A flight of steps goes to a second level that is open all round, and up under the spreading eaves of the delicate roof, the space gives an impress of quivering life. There is so much gold on the ceiling; so many red beams, and objects of crystal, and white shells, arching elephant tusks, and fresh white flowers heaped on gold cloths, a sweet perfume — flowers and incense; gold vases with red lilies; carved and painted guardian figures and banners, banners everywhere. All the lustre and gold light focused on this ultimate shrine could give one an exhilarating idea: it is late spring near a peach tree in full bloom and the sun in the fragrant air has turned the tree into rubies and gold.

The Tooth Relic of the Buddha is enshrined here. The shrine was built by King Vimaladharmasuriya in the 17th century when Kandy was the capital of Ceylon. King Weeraparatrama Narendrasinghe rebuilt the temple reducing it from three stories to two stories. The last King Sri Vikrama Rajasinha added the "octagon" to the shrine and built the moat on its boundary. As the tooth relic was considered the palladium of royalty the Temple of the Tooth was always built beside the King's palace. The temple has painting of the Kandyan period.

Originally on the walls of the main part of the Royal Palace building were stucco figures of chowri bearing women of nearly human size; and terracotta figures of lions and geese (Pl. 42). These beautiful figures had been covered by successive layers of lime-wash applied during the British administration. The roof of this building is in the Dutch style. The palace covered a vast area of land but no further trace of it can be found today. It was burnt and destroyed by the Portuguese and again by the English but later was rebuilt and used by them for the governor's residence.

Let us pause in our narrative for some necessary history.

The ancient superstitions were reclaimed by Buddhism since the Buddhist's duty was to free himself from the chain of existence and there was almost no religious ceremony as such. But even from Asoka's time the popular demand for shrines and monuments provided a non-intellectual strain to the Buddhist culture and its attendant sculpture and architecture. Also the religion was ready to provide political power as its instrument. The story of the national hero, Dutugamunu, shows the earliest Sinhalese nationalism and his war-cry was "not for kingdom but for Buddhism". It was these early struggles that kept the Sinhala kingdom from being absorbed by the larger expanding South Indian Tamil kingdoms. In the 13th and 14th centuries the island divided into three parts: Udarata or the Kandyan kingdom, stretching toward Batticoloa, the Kingdom of Kotte near Colombo, and the Northern, Jaffna.

In the 15th century the long reign of Parakrama Bahu VI was the last to sway the whole of Ceylon. It was a peaceful reign. In his excellent *Story of Ceylon* E.F.C. Ludowyk states:

"Though the Sinhala Kingdom declined and its kings were limited to narrower domains, the more splendid grew the religious cults with which kingdom and king were associated. The development of the cult of the Tooth Relic of the Buddha between the twelfth and sixteenth centuries, the magnificence of its rituals, the belief in its miraculous powers, the particular veneration in which it was held as an object of worship as well as guaranteeing the king his right to the kingdom, must have derived some of their fervour from desperation as well as from hope, even in periods of defeat, that magically the possession of the relic would assure the ultimate triumph of the kingdom.

"Parakrama Bahu I fought a war to gain possession of the relic without which he could not establish his right to the throne. A special bodyguard was assigned to it, magnificent temples were built in its honour, and its exposition was the occasion of spectacular ceremonies. Over the other relics of the Buddha, acquired in the course of time, there had been temples built, and festivals were instituted in their honour. But none of them, not even the branch of the Bo tree brought, according to the story, by the Theri Sanghamitta from India, has been able to conjure so much popular emotion as the celebrated Tooth Relic. It moved with the kings who set up new capitals, for without it there could be neither kingdom or king. For a short while during the first half-century of British colonial rule in the island, the colonial government was responsible for its security and the annual perahĕra or procession in its honour."

The capital of the Kandyan kingdom at its beginning was known as Senkadagalapura and later came to be known as Sri Wardhanapura, the city that increased her beauty and prosperity, or by both names combined together. But the people called it Maha Nuwara or the great city because it was the capital of the kingdom with the ruling monarch residing there. It had the Satara Wahalkada or the four gates, the guard-houses facing the four quarters of the city thus enabling the soldiers to guard and protect the central nucleus of power.

The city having been founded and the royal palace built by King Vikramabahu III of Gangasiripura (Gampola), the first King to ascend the throne of Senkadagalapura was Senna Sammata Vikramabahu. When Vimaladharmasuriya I ascended the throne in the city of Sri Wardhana in 1592 AD he surrounded the whole of the vast city with a massive wall on the top of which he had placed at intervals eighteen towers, and then to ward off the foe, he posted sentries and, it was said, freed the whole Kingdom of Lanka from all oppression. After his decisive battle fought against the Portuguese at Danture the victorious monarch returned to the city with the captive princess Dona Catherina as his queen. He improved the city and his palace using the skills of the captured Portuguese warriors and soon the city of Sri Wardhana became the capital of the Kanda Udarata Rajadhaniya the Kingdom of the hills. The Sacred Tooth Relic was brought back to the city from Delgamuwa Vihara in the Sabaragamuwa province. The King built a two-storeyed temple on an exquisitely beautiful piece of ground in the neighbourhood of the royal palace situated just opposite his royal palace. Thus this most sacred and venerated temple of the Buddhists became an integral part of the royal palace, as was always the case from the time of the earliest Sinhalese Kings.

To Major Willerman who entered the city in 1815 it was a magnificent city in some respects. John Davy writing about Maha Nuwara in 1821 says:

"The houses which constitute the streets are all of clay of one storey, standing on a low terrace of clay, and are all thatched, with the exception of the dwellings of the chiefs, which are tiled, in brief they are all constructed on the plan described when treating the buildings in general of the natives. The only street that requires particular mention is Astawanka Weediya as we call it, Malabar Street — having been exclusively inhabited by Malabars, relatives and dependents of the King...

''The principal objects in Kandy worthy of any notice are the palace, and the different temples of Boodhoo (Buddha) and the gods. The palace did occupy a considerable space of ground. Its front, above 200 yards long, made rather an imposing appearance, it looked towards the principal temples, and rose above a handsome moat, the walls of which were pierced with triangular cavities for purpose of illuminations.''

Dalada Maligawa was first named Dalada-ge meaning the House of the Tooth Relic. Later people called it the Dalada Maligawa or Palace of the Tooth Relic, in keeping with the Sinhalese name for the Raja Maligawa (Royal Palace), and its situation in the midst of the royal buildings. The temple was originally built in two storeys by Vimaladharmasuriya I (1592-1603 AD) the remains of which are no longer extant. Vimaladharmasuriya II (1687-1707 AD) then erected a three storeyed building to house the Tooth Relic.

We now come to the upper chamber. There are three rooms in it. The first and second are called Kunama or Sandalwood shed corresponding to a perfumed chamber. It is in the first room that the exposition of the Tooth Relic from time to time takes place. The third room is the Vedahitina Maligawa where the Tooth Relic resides. The door frames of this section are inlaid with carved ivory.

There are seven golden caskets enclosing the Tooth Relic, each casket studded with precious stones. The outermost casket is adorned with jewellery offered to the relic by pious Kings and other dignitaries from time to time. On the right hand side of the Tooth Relic casket is the Perahera Karanduwa, the casket taken in the Perahera. Also there was the relic casket presented by the Government of India along with the Buddha relics from Dharmarajika Stupa in Taxila, which is now kept in the Great Treasure Room. The whole is covered by a glass case.

Mangul Maduwa

The sadistic last King of Kandy was Sri Vikrama Rajasinha, but he excelled nevertheless as a landscape architect. Any number of the good things in Kandy were his doing: the lake and crenelated walls, the moat, the big octagon buildings by the Temple of the Tooth and the charming white pavilion by the lake — the Queen's Bath. One of his achievements was to complete the Royal Audience Hall, the Mangul Maduwa, near the big Temple.

The Hall is serene and beautiful. The roof, long and spare, is the end-product of two or three thousand years of learning how best to put together a tropical wood roof. It is supported on a forest of columns spaced in rows (Pls. 43, 44). In the wet tropics, the less wall the better — columns will carry the load alone whenever privacy does not matter, and these columns are turned into works of art. Their placing gives the illusion of spaces separated by invisible walls much the way plantings of trees set garden spaces apart. By columns and air-borne roof the architect, Devendra Mulachariya, turned a hillside into a regal building. Two hundred years before us, he had walked to the outlying temples and ambalama we had seen. At Embekke he had gathered the seeds of wood-craft mastery carried up from the Old Kingdoms, and with royal patronage, produced this regal building. The work on it commenced in 1784 during the reign of King Rajadhiraja Singhi but could not be completed before the British came into possession. The building is a spacious hall having wood pillars rising from a stereobate of stone. The wood pillars are capped by carved wood brackets and are adorned by a variety of carvings. The rafters have their undersides cut into shapely curves. The roof has a steep gradient and is clad with flat tiles.

Queen's Bath

This building on the fringe of the Kandy tank is known as the bathing palace of the Queen. The verandah of its ground floor runs round three sides. The ground floor is paved with bricks and the upper floor consists of boards laid on beams. The roof of the building has the steep gradient popular in Kandyan times and is clad with flat tiles. This building which was destroyed during the Kandyan wars was rebuilt by the British for the library.

Across the lake from the Queen's Bath is the Malwatte Monastery, housing about 40 persons and providing a school (Pl. 47).

Roofs

We were drawn again to the Audience Hall summing up our speculations on how those huge dagobas on the northern plains were roofed. The little four-square roofs over small hill country dagobas would never have done the job. And, another question about the circles of stone pillars round the great domes of the North...were they really placed in logical positions for supporting roofs? Were the pillars intended for roofs at all? Perhaps they carried ornamental lintels and the circle simply outlined the ambulatory space around the dome. Considering the ring of graduated columns about the Dagoba of the Collar Bone for example, the pillared walk alone may have been roofed, becoming a covered ambulatory circle — the dome looming nobly from the centre. Or perhaps stone basins — lamps with oil and wick, may have capped the columns for lighting the domes at night. Old texts say that the earliest dagobas were actually built with niches for lamps: in some cases the blocks were laid up with each brick angle turned out and oil lamps put on their points, so at night the dagoba glowed like a half moon. Then there is the climate: the plains are dry most of the year, the winter monsoons do not last long; it is in fact quite possible the dagobas were not roofed at all. There was really no need for it. But there was an undeniable need for roofs on the houses and mansions and palaces of the cities. That is the place for roofs in scenes of the Old Kingdoms, the landscape we see today may be much as it was, but made more beautiful than by the silhouettes of steeply double-pitched roofs rising among the domes, roofs like those at Embekke and the Audience Hall. Anuradhapura and Polonnaruwa spread perhaps like forests on the plains, tropical cities of winging roofs.

Under the roof of the Kandy Audience Hall birds, bees and butterflies sailed in and out. We watched a monkey swing up a column as much at ease as in a wild forest. It would have been like this in the cities of the Old Kingdoms (Pl. 45).

EPILOGUE

A DAY'S LIFE IN KANDY

by Emily Polk

An almost inaudible sound wakes us in the night at Castle Hill — it seems to be night, black and absolutely silent but for the sound, though the clock dial shows 4.45 AM. The sound, a humming chord based on fifths, grows clearer but is still far away, and sounds as 'amber' against the 'topaz' for women's voices. The 'amber' hum begins to flex up and down, modulating and transposing through minor keys, then the tenors rise a fifth; after a few breaths the bases drop and hold; the contratenors soar off to their own realm leaving the baritones strong at centre, and we are hearing the tremendous Brahmanic dawn anthem, Gayatri, in praise of the Shining Ones. Being new to the steep slope below the wilderness, we let the enchantment of our first dawn crystallise into a ritual, and every morning began at 4.45. In a few days we realised the dawn anthem was 'canned' and the charm was rubbed off by that knowledge, but the habit remained.

Five am: Tea on the stone bench above the steep grassy bank near our verandah. In the dark before dawn the magpie robin sings from the top twig of the acacia trilling a long banner of notes that are a melodious variation of his Sinhalese name, polkichchia (we pretend sometimes he sings Polk-I-s-see-ya!). So high they are barely visible, ranks of fruit bats, black against black, stream west for a day's sleep in the forest. With the calm turning of the earth the sky lightens, shaping the dark hills; puffs of cloud blush, and the lake takes on a shine. Across the lake the big pale wings hovering in the air are the temple roofs against the hill shadows. Clusters of blossoms on the frangipani trees below us catch the glow and turn to bundles of stars in the dark. The lake reflects pink sky, hills become banks of blue mist; the temple turns violet then pink as the hills turn green. A lorry clatters along the street on the town side of the lake; the water cart grinds up our hill taking a day's supply to the houses above pump range on the edge of the wild forest up top. Traffic growls to life round about the town, and a few health buffs pace the lakeside trail.

Six am: Tom-toms tap out the slow rhythm of the first ceremony of the day across at the Temple as sunrays splash on the highest tree crowns and the temple roofs. It gilds our Amherstia nobilis, the exotic specimen tree hung with panicles of red orchid-like flowers, and strikes fire from polkichchia's diamond tones where he's top bird on the acacia, a rare variety of the tree that blooms every three or four months with large yellow flowers and apparently delicious; nimble chipmunks and epicurean birds eat the flowers. Now the sun is out, orioles fly through the trees, and tiny metallic blue-black sun-birds tilt into the flower cups probing with long curved bills for insects in nectar. Down in the lakeside trees the crows stretch and grumble, then rag off to cadge a spot of breakfast. Our paid day-boarder crows, glossy, handsome Sri Lanka birds unlike the usual scruffy run, sail into the frangipanis along the drive at the base of our garden slope and bounce down among the flowers and shrubs bordering the side that drops off toward the lake. The town is in full sun now and the twin peaks north of the beautiful valley are pale silver against the blue.

Seven am: The clear air seems perfectly still, not a leaf moves but we can smell the perfume of the frangipani flowers — the cool night air has warmed and is lifting along the hills. A few butterflies float up the slope. Now they're coming in scores; companies of yellow and white with a sprinkling of large blacks all rising bouyantly up hill, wafted by an up-draught over the trees of the drive, up the grassy bank, sail past the house and around our bench, lift again over the boulders and vines of the hill behind and out of sight on their way to the wild land above. Every morning they come swinging up. The valley air rises so delicately not a spider web sways but the butterflies ride a slow irresistible current.

Eight am: The gardener is at work trimming shrubs. Two of his boys mow the lawn on the steep drop near the verandah; one boy as anchorman holds a rope up top and the other works the securely tied mower down to the flat bit of lawn below. They join the gardener who is striding up the slope towards us with a broad smile. The boys laugh and point to his head. A five inch twig with a few dry leaves is attached to his turban, but the cause of the excitement escapes us until we see the twig move, leaves and all. It stretches out stiff hair-thin arms and legs, and clambers jerkily down the gardener's shoulders and arms. One of the boys takes it to march up his arm, and they want to know if we'd like to have it. No, we say, the rare insect should be put back among the flowers, and we lead the procession to place it with much ceremony on a tangle of vines, and presto! it has vanished. Not even the gardener's sharp eyes can find it again.

Nine am: The three hills of Kandy take different shapes: the one behind the Temple is a big loaf with horizontal contours: the west hill is higher with broad shoulders; and our hill, on the south, spreads like a fan with ravines making the pleats. All three hills are wooded. The road on our hillside dips in, out and sharply around, and only a few cars come along. Those that do we can hear coming from two ravines away, so the road is a friendly track. We stroll down our drive and take a walk on the hill road, walking slowly. We and the old men out for a stroll are the only ones walking slowly, the housewives all walk quickly carrying baskets and bright coloured umbrellas, made in Japan to keep off the sun.

The old paper parasol is impractical in the rain-prone hills; the children are your world-round children, running skipping, dragging and so on. We notice people detouring round a patch of the road — when we reach it we detour too; a dark green scorpion as long as a dinner knife is crossing at a businesslike pace. Everyone is careful not to disturb him; every living thing on this island has a place in the scheme of things.

Ten am: The road we are on is called Raja Pihilla Mawatha, the King's Bath Road. We've been mystified by the name; there is usually some basis for a name as specific as that. We walk along going east and speculate if up top in the wild forest where maps show a spot marked 'Reservoir' there may be the ruins of a royal bath. Suggestions made by us from time to time that we investigate up there are quashed. By no means were we to go near the wilds; we were advised not even to walk up the roads that lead to the high ground. Dangers were only too real, we were told, snakes especially, and foxes. Did they mean jackals? No, no, foxes, very fierce foxes. We see no reason to refine the matter and stay on the lower hillside. Cliffs overhang the road in places, and trees wound with creepers, shrubs and vines are so dense we see merely inches into this overflow from the hilltop; the road seems wild enough even with glimpses of houses tucked into woods. Rounding a 'pleat' the ravine beyond was more open than most and we hear the sound of water, of dashing water and through the trees we see a marvellous sight: cascades and waterfalls splash down between and over the boulders of a wide, leafy watercourse. Stones built into platforms held pools. We can see for several hundred feet up the gently slope of the ravine, and people are bathing up there. A few laughing lads splash water at each other; their clothes were draped on the stones. A culvert carried the stream under the road and downhill a series of big tubs were lined up, the water flowing from one to the next. A woman and two men slosh and bang clothes beside the tubs — dhobies. Below the road, water is business; but the up-road side. Was this echoing, water-spangled hideaway the place of the King's Bath in the old days? If the artistic tyrant, Sri Vikrama Rajasinha, had come this way, we could very well be looking at the plumbing for the Raja Pihilla itself.

Eleven am: Outside our gates the road west swings sharply left down to a small temple-school where children in white uniforms sit in a pavilion beside a dagoba and chant their lessons. Across from the school in the Royal Park, at one time a pleasure grove from the Kandyan kings, a cannon from the Second World War is raised on a flower-banked mound. The piece is a gift from Lord Mountbatten whose headquarters was nearby. On down the steep road some very tall trees grow on the uphill cliff. We are on our way to the town, and rounding the curve we see a troop of monkeys in a death-defying game. Apparently they have come via tree-tops to these three favourite trees that may be 80 feet tall, the lower 60 feet are limbless and solidly wrapped with the thick stems and huge leaves of the elephant-ear vine. The troop is plunging down the vine-covered trunks of all three trees, hand over foot over head over heel over tail at high speed in an every-which-way monkey waterfall, grasping the vine just often enough to break their drop and keep from flying off into space. The three trees are three monkey-cascades. At the top infant monkeys practise on bending limbs and a few teenagers swing expertly 80 feet up. But their elders have mastered the fine art of vine-diving and are having the time of their lives.

Ibn Batuta, the adventurous Moor of 1344, has a tall story about the monkeys. "These animals are very numerous in the mountains: they are of black colour and have long tails. Those of the male sex have beards like men. (Persons) have related to me that the monkeys have a Chief whom they obey like a Sovereign. He binds round his head a wreath of the leaves of trees, and supports himself with a staff. Four monkeys, bearing staves, march on his right and left, and when the chief is seated, they stand behind him. His wife and little ones come and sit before him every day. The other monkeys come and squat at some distance; each brings a banana or a lime or some fruit. The king of the monkeys, his little ones, and the four chief monkeys then eat." If there was a descendant from that monkey king we saw him one day with his family doing a high-wire act on the telephone line as a short-cut over the road. The male went ahead, the others followed, one by one on all fours gripping the line with intense concentration. This practice wrecks the telephone connections and since repairs take forever, people discourage a visitation of monkeys with whatever comes to hand. When 'phones don't work it's usually blamed on monkeys; they are not universally popular in the hills.

Eleven-thirty am: On our way to Cargills to look over their new shipment of 'European' supplies, sherry, cornflakes, etc, we turned a corner at the same time as an elephant. One doesn't think of elephants as townies, but this chap had just parked his salad in the car park between the Fiats (the greens were roughly the same size as the cars), and was off on an errand with his mahout in tow. He waited for traffic, then stalked along as confident as an M.P. (Pl. 46).

Returning home we crossed the causeway of Kandy Lake. The old name of Kandy Lake was Kiri Muhuda, the Milky Sea. The colour of the water is light green rather like the River Nile or cloudy emeralds. From Castle Hill we can see dark forms moving underwater...submerged logs? But they rose to the surface and indistinct arms and legs showed them to be enormous lizards. Some of the lizards are said to be 14 feet long eating only fish eggs and water weeds. The dark bodies cruise at varying depths, each one alone until the spring mating season; they move towards one another then with a rather ominous fixity of purpose, and after a half hour of slow-motion courtship roll wildly, churning a froth on the Milky Sea. The lake is commonly believed to be haunted. No one swims in it. Schools of fish ripple on the water and people throw food to them but no one fishes. A crenelated wall runs along the town side of the lake and in the late afternoon people gather to gossip and visit and toss scraps to the fish. Droves of fish congregate for handouts, all layered to size: small silver ones near the surface, below them are the large pinks, then huge carp-like shadows, in the deeps.

One pm: In the centre of the patio off the dining room there is a roomy, roofed, chicken-wire-walled, trumpet-vine and orchid- covered bird house. A young grackle has lived there a week. He clings to the wire, swivelling his red and yellow head to follow the two wild grackles that have been flying about the place and calling. They may be his parents. When the wild ones are out of sight and sound, the grackle settles down and digs into the pawpaw pushed through the wire or eats the orchid flowers. He's learned to cry 'bhad ghow', Sinhalese for 'give rice'! and everyone is delighted. Today at lunch we notice the bird has learned to fly properly for the first time. He swoops across the cage in top form with a good pounce at the end. He looks much too strong for the rickety old cage.

Two pm: Great excitement and shouting — the grackle has escaped. How no one knows. Some think the gardener felt sorry for him and let him out, but others say he slipped through a crack on the roof. The shouting dies down and we go out to sit on the verandah and suddenly hear grackles calling from the acacia where they've not come before. We run out and look – there they are, three brilliant heads and glistening black wings among the yellow flowers. They sweep into the air and put on a stunning aerial display over the house and back again and away. We hear their whistling cries mount on the airway to the wilds; a deep forest tone and as one might imagine the cry of the last pterodactyl, or some other lost bird-spirit.

Three-thirty pm: It's become an afternoon of sun and brief showers and now an extraordinary rainbow, a small brilliant bow no higher than the valley. One end rests on a point of our hill east of us, and the other plunges into the lake. So the rainbow and its reflection are a complete circle.

Five pm: A few minutes ago the brahminy kite made his last headlong fishing dive of the day. The crows are now chivvying him all the way to the hill; in a little while they'll return and join their five hundred brothers settled for the night in the lake trees, and all sing their roosting songs, ear-splitting at close range, but up here at tea time their caws come as a long-growled cello to polkichchia's violin.

The marvellous polkichchia not only makes music but dances a particularly witty evening revue in black tie. He flutters and somersaults mid-air catching insects. The steam-whistle screams, overhead are homing parakeets shrieking farewell to the sun. Kandy sunsets drive sunset collectors to a frenzy of photography. The whole field of the sky pulses with shades of gold, apricot pink and mauve, and here and there a pure white cloud looms into the porcelain-blue scraps of the day.

Here high on the island the winds from the Bay of Bengal and the Indian Ocean are on a collision course. Cloud fleets sail from the north-east, slow down and stop; a counter wind captures them and sails them back again. At times white cumulus mounds drift west, and below them near the hills long ragged, gray banners are streaming east. If the sun is setting when clouds battle, the sensation of colours, movement and light is electrifying. One feels slightly hysterical; the sun plays the colours so fast you can't blink or you'll miss some even wilder splendour: the subtleties rally and fade in a wink.

Six pm: The sun is leaving the stage with a fanfare of flaming colours and the first of the great fruit bats heads east across the evening sky. Before full dark hundreds of them will fly over us at a deliberate pace that carries them twenty miles or more to their feeding ground for the night. On the ceiling of the verandah a gecko chuckles in a rapid tapping that sounds like someone rapping on glass with a stone. As far as we know Sri Lanka geckos are the only ones that chuckle — and we don't blame them.

Six-thirty pm: Their evening's web-spinning on the verandah bamboo completed, the small spiders inspect and tighten a few strands and then settle at centre to see what the night brings. After the showers tree frogs have tuned up, scattered small voices very like the tinkle of ice cubes in a glass. We've been lavish with our mosquito sticks and relax without misgivings enjoying the loveliness of the evening, the clear sky and a few early stars. Rasaiah came to the verandah a moment ago to take the tea things and as he reached for the tray we exclaimed "Look! Look at the sky!"

Rasaiah glances at what we see then jumps back with a startled word in Sinhalese: in the star-pricked sky two large round luminous circles one larger than the full moon are poised high above the hills, shimmering with rainbow stripes. The smaller one, somewhat flattened at the sides, seems further away to the north, as if near the twin peaks. The larger is about two hands above the central point of the Temple hill. We look at the clock, "just twenty to seven!"

While we are staring at the two pulsing lights, without an instant's warning a third light is there, east of the others — a flame-red disc of shimmers and flows. The edges undulate and quiver. In a minute the orange colour slowly begins to change to blues at the edge and, colour by colour, with many quivering undulations resolves into the rainbow stripes of the other two. The stripes of all three are just off vertical and their shape slightly ovoid giving the impression that viewed from true west, they would be true circles with vertical bands of colour. The sun is far below the horizon now. Only an orange glow outlines the west hills. For fifteen or twenty minutes the discs quiver and pulse then begin delicately to fade from the centres outward, and, keeping the circular form, extend out all around getting fainter and fainter until there are only stars in the clear sky.

Seven pm: Rasaiah sits transfixed on the low wall of the verandah. "Have you seen this before?" His eyes shine with excitement. "No, never. Unknown things."

Still spellbound we walk on the lawn to bring us back to earth. Tree frogs tinkle and clink, night blooming jasmines smell sweeter than incense, and the sky is a fireworks of stars. We turn back toward the house and at the far end of the lawn, the acacia is now a tall tracery of black. Cool lights flicker in hundreds through the tree, and hover on the tips of invisible branches: the evening fireflies. The tree is white with sparks. Some swing out against the sky, diamond points just like the stars, but the fireflies dance.

Eight-thirty pm: Later tonight the full moon should be up but it has started to rain again so we won't see it, and the small perahera, due

for 9 o'clock, will be a wet one. Full moon day and night is a holiday
every month in Sri Lanka in memory of the Buddha's enlightenment
on the night of the full moon of May about 528 BC. He had been
practising austerities sitting by the river when Mara approached with
his horde of demons and said, "You are emaciated, pale, you are near
death. Live, Sir, life is better. Do meritorious deeds. What is the use of
striving?" Gautama replied, "Lust is your first army; the second is
dislike for higher life; the third is hunger and thirst; the fourth is
craving; the fifth is torpor and sloth; the sixth is cowardice; the seventh
is doubt; the eighth is hypocrisy and obduracy; the ninth is gains,
pride, honour, false glory; the tenth is exalting self and despising
others. Mara, these are your armies. No feeble man can conquer them,
yet only by conquering them one wins bliss. I challenge you! Shame on
my life if defeated! Better for me to die in battle than to live defeated..."
Mara, dejected and overcome with grief, disappeared. Gautama then
spent the rest of the full moon night deep in meditation. In the first
watch from 6 pm to 10 he learned of his former existences. In the
middle watch from 10 to 2 am he attained the power to see the passing
away and rebirth of beings. In the last watch from 2 am to 6 he gained
knowledge of the destruction of all defilements and realised the Four
Noble Truths; and later he said "My mind was emancipated...Ignorance
was dispelled, knowledge arose; darkness was dispelled, light arose."

The Old Kingdoms reckoned time on a lunar calendar, and not
until trade and business required a reckoning less erratic was the solar
calendar adopted; but not for Buddhist affairs, these matters are still
anchored to the moon. Most businesses close on full moon day,
everyone dresses at his best and takes flowers to the temple, and many
spend the day on the temple grounds visiting and listening to monks
chant the words of the Buddha. Kandy-towners and tourists go to
Natha Devale square and the Temple of the Tooth. The scene at the
square stirs together a heady potion for visitors, a cocktail made of
nostalgic tones of flutes, hypnotic drums and chanting, and the heavy
sweet smell of temple flowers.

The big event, the spectacle of spectacles in Kandy, is the Perahera
of the August Moon already noted. After William Hull saw it in 1955 he
wrote what he felt and 'said it all': "The Kandy perahera, in part for its
beautiful transcendence of barbarism, is what every alien should be
urged to come to see. One's first and lasting impression is of the
quietness of the people who pour in early day by day, sit, eat, wait,
drink, sit: the Perahera explodes in majesty; the people sit and watch
from their bellies; the Perahera is done: the people quietly, without

pushing, vanish. It is possible that the Kandy perahera is the most deeply moving feudal procession left in this one world...The incremental tempo, night by night; the deep dignity of processional renewal of one's cultural fundaments; the focussing in the dancer, the gorgeous and stately civic figure, and the elephant, of all one's personal and communal memory, need, and desire are to an alien not only moving but renewing."

Hundreds of elephants parade in the big Perahera, each temple of the Kandy District sends elephants in full dress with light-bulb masks (concealed batteries are on their backs), and groups of drummers and dancers. The largest elephant in the District belongs to the Temple of the Tooth, he has the honour of carrying the Tooth Relic in its nest of gold caskets. Dancers wearing demon masks and feathered headdresses build a convincing frenzy. The show, so wonderfully archaic, is an anomaly of Buddhism.

When the Perahera is over two strictly 20th century demons stay on to challenge Buddhist serenity and the 2600 year-old rituals: electronic amplification and pre-recording. The fine-tuned balance between the natural volume of singers' voices, the drums and the sensibilities of the devotees achieved over those ages, is in gravest danger: amplification knocks out a religious mood, and any feeling of an imminent 'presence' is gone in the blast. Pre-recording is a glib substitute of machined emotion for the sung spirit, and, the exquisite dawn hymn palls when it comes on inhumanly the same, morning after morning. We can only hope Buddhist purists will come down heavily on these innovations. A prime quality of Sri Lanka is the perfection of tradition. One listens to the tom-toms (unamplified) from the Temple early in the morning and it's 2300 years ago — Sri Lanka undertook to guard the fundamentals of Buddha's message, and now Mara's 9th army is on the attack with an array of hi-tech vanities.

Nine pm: Raining hard now. From our window we see the Temple lights go on. Torch bearers come down the steps and swing into the street, then dancers fall in behind them with their drumming team, then an elephant pivots slowly down the steps and lines up;...another contingent of torches, dancers, drummers; another elephant...three sets of people and elephants...the rainy perahera parades along beside the lake with the double glitter of torches reflected in the wet street; and from our hill we see another bright wet procession drifting along upside down in the black water of the lake.

GLOSSARY

ambamama: rest house
dagoba, stupa: edifice built over a relic, generally dome-shaped
devale, vihara: Buddhist shrine, temple
digge: fore-porch for temple ceremony, often for drums
garbhagriha: sanctum
perahera: religious procession
pekada: column bracket
sikhara: temple spire
stereobate: plinth
torana: temple gateway
vihara: see devale

NOTES

The Bo-tree is a pipul tree (Ficus religiosa).
There are three principal palms in Sri Lanka: arecanut, coconut, toddy.
The stick insect described is a Phasmida.
Wood scorpion: Heterometrus.
Elephant ear vine: Philodendron giganteum.
Monitor lizard: Veranus salvador.

BIBLIOGRAPHY

"Some Aspects of Stupa Symbolism", Anagarika K. Govinda, Kitabistan, Allahabad and London, 1940

"Wooden Architecture of Sri Lanka", L.K. Karunaratne, The Ceylon Historical Journal, October 1978

"The Stupa in Ceylon", S. Paranavitana, Memoirs of the Archaeological Survey of Ceylon, Colombo, 1946

"Sri Lanka and Monsoon Asia: Patterns of Local and Regional Architectural Development and the Problem of the Traditional Sri Lankan Roof", S. Bandaranayake, Parana Vitana Commemoration Volume, Brill, 1978

A History of Sri Lanka, K.M. De Silva, University of California Press, 1981

Mediaeval Sinhalese Art, A.K. Coomaraswamy, New York, 1956

Sinhalese Monastic Architecture, S. Bandaranayake, Leiden, 1974

"The Temple of the Tooth in Kandy", A.M. Hocart, Memoirs of the Archaeological Survey in Ceylon, Vol. IV, 1931

Buddhism, Christmas Humphreys, Pelican

Description of the Buddhist Kingdom, ancient text translated by Rumusat, Paris

On a Sojourn on the Island of Sri Lanka, William Hull, 1956, Times of Ceylon Annual

The Pearl of India, Ballou, Houghton Mifflin, 1894

The Asian Journal of Thomas Merton, 1973

Indika, the Country and People of India and Ceylon, J.F. Hurst, Harper, 1891

A World Pilgrimage, J.H. Barrows, McClurg, Chicago, 1897

Journal Letters from the Orient, Plimpton Press, 1934

Historical Relations of Ceylon, Robert Knox, 1681

The Art of Memory, Francis Yates, 1966

Diversions of a Diplomat in Sri Lanka, P.K. Crowe, Van Nostrand, 1956

Images of Sri Lanka Through American Eyes, H.A.I. Goonetileke, Embassy of the United States, 1976

The Story of Ceylon, E.F.C. Ludowyk, London, 1962

Temples of South India, section on Kerala and South Kanara, Govt. of India, Publications Division, March 1960

"The Ruins of Ancient Ceylon", Rhoads Murphey, Journal of Asian Studies, Vol. XVI, Pt. 2, 1952

Travels of Ibn Batuta in India and Ceylon, translated by Sir Albert Grey, Defremery and Sanguinetti, 1883

My Pilgrimage to the Wise Men of the East, D.C. Moncure, 1900

And many references in the writings of Professor Anuradha Seneviratna for UNESCO, the Sri Lanka Government, and others on special fields of Sri Lankan culture, for example: "The Architectural History of the Temple of the Tooth"; "Historical Monuments of Kandy"; "The Golden Rock Temple of Dambulla"; "Traditional Dance of Sri Lanka".

LIST OF PLATES

1. In stone and brick: an exceptional transplant from South India, Gadaladeniya is not typical of the Kandyan Hills.

2. A stern image in meditation, the Buddha at Gadaladeniya.

3. Is this roof at Gadaladeniya a clue to the ancient sky-lines of Anuradhapura?

4. A brick masonry structure has been transformed over the centuries by a Kandy style roof, timber-framed and tiled. Lankatilaka Temple.

5. Buddha image and the imaginary animals of the makara torana, Lankatilaka.

6. View through the columns of the digge space showing carved pekadas. Embekke Devale.

7. A skilfully crafted system of beams and rafters with central connection pin. Embekke Devale.

8. Ornament grows out of eave structure requirements. Embekke Devale.

9. Storage bins, each on four crossing beams with wattle-and-daub walls and tiled roof. Embekke.

10. A holiday at Alutnuwara. The entrance pavilion.

11. She placed one yellow flower on the shrine. Alutnuwara.

12. The infamous king Sri Vikrama Rajasinha. One wall of the muralled temple fore-space. Dodantale Vihara.

13. A concert on a hand-crafted flute. Dodantale.

14. End of the long covered footbridge at Bogoda Vihara.

15. Polk at the Bogoda footbridge. Baluster ornament grows from structure.

16. Columns and eave with drip-tiles, temple porch, Badulla.

17. A procession in progress. Murals at Badulla.

18. Elephants, priests, and kings. A religious procession. Mural at Badulla.

19. Snake, eagle, and masked figure. Badulla mural.

20. Climax of the structural silhouette. High sanctuary roofs, Maha Saman Devale, Ratnapura.

21. Portion of exterior mural. How much more could be recovered? Maha Saman Devale, Ratnapura.

22. Seventeen foot single slab banquet table. Walawwa of Ekneligoda.

23. A small but classic Kandyan structure. The Medawala Vihara.

24. The Monk's house verandah, Ridi Vihara. Anuradha Seneviratna on left.

25. Fore-court to Cave Temple (dedicated to snakes we were told). Ridi Vihara.

26. Library, Padeniya. The interior develops split-level planning arrangements.

27. Under the eaves of the Vihara is seen the procession of lions. Padeniya Vihara.

28. Vibrant colour and design in inner entrance to sanctuary, Padeniya.

29. Beam on stone construction, Kolambagama Vihara.

30. A strong Buddha in folk art. Kolambagama.

31. Small temple reaching for the trees. Dorbawila Vihara.

32. Well-integrated eave, baluster, and floor cantilever. Dorbawila Vihara.

33. Entrance to sanctum with plinth bas-reliefs and entrance guardian images. Niyamgampaya Vihara.

34. A light structure from heavy timbers. The Godamunne Ambalama.

35. Looking down to courtyard of Dodanwela Vihara. Notice decorative roof tiles.

36. Wood roof over masonry stupa. Gedige Vihara, Kandy.

37. Ceremonial gateway. The roof was added later. Natha Devale, Kandy.

38. The Dalada Maligawa as it stands today, seen from the Palace Square, Kandy.

39. Detail prior to restoration work. Temple of the Tooth, Kandy.

40. Eave detail at entrance of the Temple of the Tooth, Kandy.

41. Balustrade and brilliant painted eave, Temple of the Tooth, Kandy.

42. Terracotta figures. A fragment of the ancient Royal Palace entrance. Kandy.

43. Tile patterns on the Kandyan roof of the Royal Audience Hall, Kandy.

44. Ornamental wood columns related to those at Embekke. Royal Audience Hall (Mangul Maduwa), Kandy.

45. Under the typical steep Kandyan roof structure. Royal Audience Hall, Kandy.

46. We turned a corner at the same time as an elephant carrying his lunch.

47. Lakeside schools, Malwatte Monastery across the water from the Temple of the Tooth. Kandy.

48. Looking north from our Castle Hill Guest House, Kandy.

INDEX